(Sandy)

ENGLISH FOR INTERNATIONAL
TOURISM

PETER STRUTT

Pearson Education Limited
Edinburgh Gate
Harlow
Essex CM20 2JE
England
and Associated Companies throughout the world.

www.pearsonelt.com

© Pearson Education Limited 2013

First published 2013

ISBN: Coursebook and DVD-ROM Pack
9781447923916

Printed by Neografia in Slovakia
Set in Avenir Light 9.5/12.5pt

Acknowledgements

The publishers and authors would like to thank Dorling Kindersley for permission to use authentic material taken from the Eyewitness Travel Guides.

The publishers and authors would like to thank the following people and institutions for their feedback and comments during the development of the material:

Italy: Lesley Jane Ray, Caroline Jordan; **Poland:** Jolanta Regucka-Pawlina (Cracow University of Economics), Agnieszka Rutkowska (Poznan University of Technology); **Serbia:** Zorica Kovačević (IH Belgrade Syllabus); **Spain:** María Amparo González Rúa (Escuela Universitaria de Turismo de Asturias), María del Mar González Chacón (Escuela Universitaria de Turismo de Asturias); **Russia:** Tatyana Yefremtseva (Russian International Academy for Tourism).

'DK' and the DK 'open book' logo are trade marks of Dorling Kindersley Limited and are used in this publication under licence.

Author Acknowledgements

We are grateful to the following for permission to reproduce copyright material:

Tables
Table Unit1.1 adapted from http://www.nationmaster.com/graph/eco_tou_arr_by_reg_of_ori_eur-tourist-arrivals-region-origin-europe, World Tourism Organization Statistics Database and Yearbook | United Nations World Tourism Organization; Table Unit1.3 adapted from http://www.statcan.gc.ca/tables-tableaux/sum-som/l01/cst01/arts34-eng.htm

Text
Article Unit1.2 adapted from http://www.tourism.australia.com/en-au/research/5236_6563.aspx, Tourism Australia; Article Unit5. adapted from www.terminalu.com/editors-column/what-makes-a-good-airport-and-why-many-have-got-it-wrong/15594/, Louise Driscoll; Extract Unit5.6 adapted from http://www.iom-airport.com/customer/safety.xml, Isle of Man Government ©2012 Crown Copyright

In some instances we have been unable to trace the owners of copyright material, and we would appreciate any information that would enable us to do so.

Illustration Acknowledgments

(Key: b-bottom; c-centre; l-left; r-right; t-top)

Tony Richardson 55, 57

Picture Credits

The publisher would like to thank the following for their kind permission to reproduce their photographs:

(Key: b-bottom; c-centre; l-left; r-right; t-top)

akg-images Ltd: Erich Lessing 58bc, Francis Frith Collection 8t, North Wind Picture Archives 58cr; **Alamy Images:** Blue Jean Images 14br, Caro 16t, David Levenson 64t, Don B. Stevenson 40t, Garry Gay 59c, Greg Balfour Evans 54r, Inspirestock Inc 73tr, J W Alker / imagebroker 41cl, John Kellerman 27b, Markus Keller / imagebroker 86bl, Thomas Cockrem 41tr, UpperCut Images 37tr, Viacheslav Khmelnytskyi 24t; **Bananastock:** 10cl, 70tl; **Bridgeman Art Library Ltd:** Eduard Hau / Hermitage, St Petersburg, Russia 54cr, John Sell / The Higgins Art Gallery & Museum, Bedford, UK 59cr, John Wycliffe, English School / Private Collection / Ken Welsh 58bl, Mitchell Library, State Library of New South Wales 58br, Pietro Antonio / State Russian Museum, St Petersburg, Russia 54l, Private Collection 59cl; **Corbis:** 89b, 41, 43, 45, 47tr, Ariel Skelley / Blend Images 72tc, Cardinal 63b, Holden Caulfield / Image Source 18tr, David Clapp / Arcaid 5tc, 54br, David Spurdens / Flame 69tr, Drew Myers / Fancy 68l, Helena Wahlman / Alloy 76bl, Image Source 21b, 32tc, Jose Luis Pelaez, Inc / Image Source 88t, Ken Seet / Comet 43b, Matthew Ashton / AMA 61b, Michael Prince / Ivy 68bl, Michael Schmeling / imagebroker 34tr, Naho Yoshizawa / Aflo 84cl, Ocean 30cr, 32bl, 74tr, Pete Oxford / Minden Pictures 35b, RelaXimages / Alloy 80t, Rick Gomez 24bl, Simon Marcus 14tr, Tim Pannell 48b, Viaframe / Crush 36t; **DK Images:** 18cr, 32cr, 38tr, 58tr, 59r, 66tr, 82tr, Clive Streeter 79tc, 79tr, Greg Ward 31tr, Leandro Zoppe 38c, Lucio Rossi 38cl, 39cl; **Fotolia.com:** 76tl, 76cl, 79t, 86t, 106tc, 16, 18, 22tl, 32, 34, 38tl, 33. 35. 37, 39tr, 61, 63, 65, 67tr, 76, 78, 82tl, 8,10,14tl, 84, 86, 90tl, 9, 11, 13, 15tr, nyul 100, travelguide 98; **Getty Images:** Brooke Slezak / The Image Bank 32l, Carlo A / Flickr 68cl, Cavan Images / Photodisc 37br, Christian Kober / AWL Images 66c, Comstock Images 81tr, Datacraft Co Ltd 20t, Dennis Barnes / Britain on View 22cr, Digital Vision 44t, Echo / Cultura 75tr, Erik Isakson 9cr, EschCollection / Photonica 46tr, Fuse 84cr, George Doyle / Stockbyte 37r, Gonzalo Azumendi / The Image Bank 52cl, Greg Elms / Lonely Planet Images 79tl, ImagesBazaar 17cr, Jeff Rotman / Photographer's Choice 84t, John Lund / Marc Romanelli 106tr, Ken Chernus / Riser 32b, Michelangelo Gratton / Digital Vision 68t, Mike Powell / Stone 70bl, Peter Walton / Photolibrary 18br, quavondo / the Agency Collection 42tc, Ray Kachatorian / Workbook Stock 75tc, Richard I'Anson / Lonely Planet Images 78c, Thomas Barwick / Iconica 60t, Tim Graham 56t, William Albert Allard / National Geographic 83b, Yuri Arcurs 60cl; **John Foxx Images:** 85, 87, 89, 91tr; **Library Hotel Collection:** 25cl; **MIXA Co Ltd:** 91bl; **Pearson Education Ltd:** 69, 71, 73, 75tr, Jules Selmes 32cl, 52, 54, 58tl; **PhotoDisc:** 77, 79, 81, 83tr; **Photolibrary.com:** 77tr; **Photoshot Holdings Limited:** WpN / UPPA 4 (film D); **Rex Features:** Sipa Press 25br, West Coast Surfer / Mood Board 70cl; **Robert Harding World Imagery:** Ben Pipe 5cl, 51b, Christian Kober 52b, Douglas Peebles 76t, Ellen Rooney 54b, Enzo Baradel / age fotostock 31c, Frans Lemmens 52t, Jeremy Bright 93b, Mark Mawson 5b, 52tl, Matthew Wakem / Aurora Photos 74-75cr, O Louis Mazzatenta / National Geographic 52l, Yadid Levy / age fotostock 54bl; **Shutterstock.com:** 37cr, 37b, 52c, 17, 19, 21, 23tr, 24, 26, 30tr, 25, 27, 29, 31tr, 40, 42, 46tl, 53, 55, 57, 59tr, 60, 62, 66tr, 68, 70, 74tl, Yuri Yavnik 5tr, 11c; **SuperStock:** Axiom Photographic Limited 12t, Bernd Rohrschneider / age fotostock 52bl, Blend Images 68b, F1 Online 82c, Hemis.fr 62cl, Juice Images 90-91, Nordic Photos 30bl, Photononstop 5cr, 41tl, Ranco Pizzochero / Marka 5tl, 95b, Tips Images 54cl, Westend61 71cr; www.imagesource.com: Cultura 28t

Cover images: *Front:* **4Corners Images:** Guido Cozzi / SIME bc, Massimo Ripani / SIME tc; **Corbis:** Blaine Harrington III b; **Getty Images:** Stuart Westmorland t; *Back:* **DK Images:** Greg Ward bl; **Robert Harding World Imagery:** Mark Mawson tl; **Shutterstock.com:** Yuri Yavnik cl

All other images © Pearson Education

In some instances we have been unable to trace the owners of copyright material, and we would appreciate any information that would enable us to do so.

INTRODUCTION

English for International Tourism is a three-level series designed to meet the English language needs of professionals working in the tourism industry and students of tourism in further education. The course includes authentic material taken from Dorling Kindersley's acclaimed *Eyewitness Travel Guides* which explore some of the world's top tourist destinations. The course helps you to:

- build confidence in professional skills such as dealing with enquiries, marketing destinations, offering advice, negotiating, writing emails and speaking to groups
- develop language awareness through an integrated grammar and skills syllabus
- acquire the specialized vocabulary needed by tourism professionals
- practise language skills in realistic Case studies that reflect issues in the tourist industry today.

Structure of the Coursebook

The Coursebook contains ten units and two Review and consolidation sections. Each unit is divided into four lessons. The Unit Menu shows you the key learning objective of the lesson. Each unit has the same structure:

- a vocabulary lesson
- a grammar lesson
- a Professional skills lesson
- a Case study or tourism-related game.

KEY VOCABULARY

The vocabulary lessons introduce and practise many words and expressions required in the tourism industry introduced through either a reading text or a listening. By the end of the lesson you will be better able to use the specialist vocabulary in appropriate tourism contexts. At the end of each unit there is a Key Word box that provides a selection of words and phrases from the unit and a reference to the Mini-dictionary on the DVD-ROM.

KEY GRAMMAR

In the grammar lessons key aspects of grammar that are essential for progress at this level are presented within an authentic tourism context. These lessons include clear explanations and activities designed to help you understand and use the language effectively. By the end of the lesson you will be able to use the grammar more confidently. For additional support there is a comprehensive Grammar reference at the back of the Coursebook.

PROFESSIONAL SKILLS

The Professional skills lessons provide you with the opportunity to learn and practise effective interpersonal and business skills which are an essential job requirement in the travel and tourism industries. You will learn professional skills ranging from dealing with customer enquiries and meeting clients' needs to preparing a guided tour or a presentation.

CASE STUDIES

Each unit ends with a Case study linked to the unit's tourism theme. The Case studies are based on realistic tourism issues or situations and are designed to motivate and actively engage you in seeking solutions. They use the language and professional skills which you have acquired while working through the unit and involve you in discussing the issues and recommending solutions through active group work.

Language skills

Speaking skills: Each unit provides you with a range of speaking activities. The pairwork tasks are designed to provide you with further opportunities to communicate in realistic and motivating tourism-related contexts. The Case studies require you to engage in extended communication about topical issues in the tourism industry. At each level further speaking practice is available in a tourism-related board game.

Listening skills: Each unit contains several listening tasks developed around topics related to the travel industry. A range of British, American and other international native and non-native speakers are featured, helping you understand how people speak English in different parts of the world. Audio scripts of the recordings are available at the back of the Coursebook.

Reading practice: Reading texts feature regularly in the units providing you with a variety of texts and topics that you are likely to encounter in a tourism context.

Writing practice: In the writing sections you will write real texts related to the tourism workplace such as emails and tour itineraries. At each level there are also writing tasks to help you get a job in tourism. Models of text types are available in the Writing Bank at the back of the Coursebook.

Workplace skills

Working with numbers: Throughout the course there are sections that help you to manipulate numbers in English, which is a vital skill in the travel and tourism workplace.

Research tasks: Each unit contains one or more research tasks that encourage you to explore tourism-related issues on the internet or in your local environment.

Private study

Workbook: A separate Workbook with a CD provides you with extra tasks for study at home or in class. There are two versions of the Workbook – one with the answer key for private study and one without a key which can be used by the teacher for extra practice in class.

DVD-ROM: The course has a DVD-ROM designed to be used alongside the Coursebook or as a free-standing video for private study. The DVD-ROM is attached to the back of the Coursebook and provides you with five authentic films featuring different aspects of tourism. Each film has a printable worksheet, a transcript and a key to the exercises. These films give you the opportunity to listen to a variety of native and non-native speakers using English as an international language in five authentic documentary videos. Additionally, the DVD-ROM has a comprehensive Mini-dictionary featuring over 300 tourism-related terms along with their definitions, pronunciation and example sentences. The DVD-ROM also contains the MP3 files of the Coursebook audio material.

Professional exams

English for International Tourism is recommended preparation for the LCCI English for tourism exams (www.lcci.org.uk).

WORLD MAP

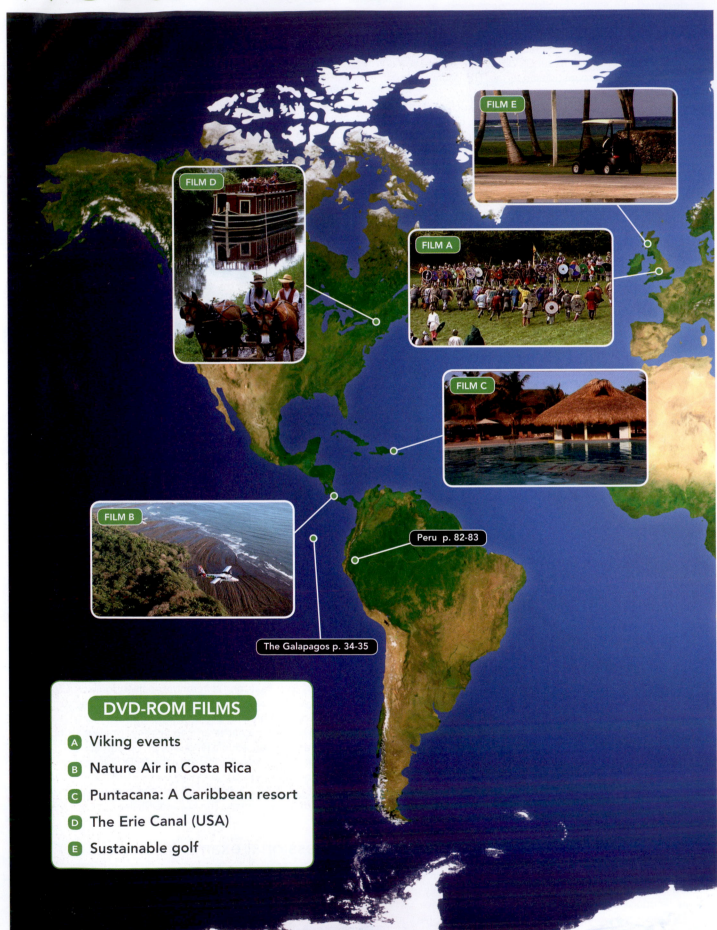

FILM E

FILM D

FILM A

FILM C

FILM B

Peru p. 82-83

The Galapagos p. 34-35

DVD-ROM FILMS

- **A** Viking events
- **B** Nature Air in Costa Rica
- **C** Puntacana: A Caribbean resort
- **D** The Erie Canal (USA)
- **E** Sustainable golf

Italy p. 94–95

China p. 10–11

St Petersburg p. 54–55

Brijuni Archipelago p. 38-39

Malaysia p. 66-67

Singapore p. 40–41

Goa p. 50–51

Sydney p. 52–53

CONTENTS

1

TRENDS IN TOURISM

UNIT MENU

Grammar: continuous aspect
Vocabulary: tourist motivations, describing visuals
Professional skills: using visuals
Case study: Getaway Travel – tailor a package

Reading

THE HISTORY OF TOURISM

1 **Read about the history of tourism and put the paragraphs in chronological order (1–6).**

A __ With a great deal of time to spend in leisure pursuits – under Emperor Claudius, there were 159 public holidays – the Roman aristocracy had ample opportunity to go out of town for pleasure and relaxation. The most popular destination was the Bay of Naples, just four days' journey from Rome down the paved Via Domitiana. With an itinerarium – a list of villages and cities and the distances between them, which could be purchased from a street vendor – visitors knew in advance what facilities their chosen accommodation offered.

B __ During the Age of the Enlightenment in the eighteenth century, it was fashionable for young aristocrats to travel around Europe for up to three years in order to visit and study great works of art and architecture and to improve their education. This was known as the Grand Tour and took place in Paris, Florence, Rome and Venice.

C __ Throughout history, people have always found reasons to travel. The Olympic Games gave the ancient Greeks an opportunity to leave home every four years to watch the competitions. They also travelled to temples erected in honour of the god of healing and medicine, in the hope of being cured.

D __ Tourism, in the modern sense, dates back to the nineteenth century, when Thomas Cook first exploited the opportunity for short organized trips. In 1845 he chartered a train and offered a 150-km excursion with pre-paid accommodation and a list of department stores to visit. It was not long before he was taking parties to Switzerland, Italy, Egypt and the United States on all-inclusive tours.

E __ The early twentieth century was the golden age for the luxury cruise industry. Places like Havana, Miami and Beirut always had a ship in port, with passengers on 'cruise and stay' voyages. But holidays abroad were still only for the affluent and it was not until the 1970s and 80s that ordinary people who wanted to get away and enjoy themselves abroad were able to do so. Mass tourism was beginning to take off.

F __ Getting from A to B in the Middle Ages was often difficult and dangerous but pilgrims traversed long distances to visit the Holy Land or famous shrines, such as the one at Santiago de Compostela in Spain, and this created a demand for inns and hostelries for an overnight stay.

2 **Read the texts in Exercise 1 again and tick (✓) the reasons for travel mentioned.**

1 __ amusement   **4** __ health   **7** __ sport

2 __ business   **5** __ religion   **8** __ visiting friends and relatives

3 __ education   **6** __ shopping

Speaking

TOURISM DEVELOPMENTS

3 In what ways do you think the tourism industry has changed since the 1970s? Discuss with a partner. Think about the factors below.

- types of holiday
- advances in technology
- choice of destinations
- choice of accommodation
- transport infrastructure
- the profile of tourists

4 Tell your partner about the holidays you had as a child and the holidays you have now. How are they different?

Listening

TOURIST MOTIVATIONS

5))) **1.1** Listen to Paul Henley, a representative of the United Nations World Tourism Organization, talking about why people travel and tick (✓) the reasons he mentions. What examples does he give of these reasons?

1 ___ to escape from their daily routine

2 ___ to find out how other people live

3 ___ to visit friends and relatives

4 ___ to realize an ambition

5 ___ to acquire social status

6))) Listen again and complete what Paul says.

1 First of all, they want to recharge their batteries, just [1]_____, chill out and then come back [2]_____.

2 A couple has been saving up for a long time in order to go on a round-the-world cruise. We could call this '[3]_____'.

3 I think people often travel to [4]_____ so that when they come back, they can [5]_____ their colleagues, friends or family.

4 I'm afraid most tourists don't actually [6]_____ with the local population, except very superficially.

7))) **1.2** Now listen to Paul talking about 'push' and 'pull' factors in tourism motivation and complete the table.

Push factors	Pull factors
	cheaper cost of living
love and romance	

Speaking

PULL FACTORS

8 Work in pairs. Discuss the pull factors that motivate tourists to come to your country.

RESEARCH

Ask members of the older generation about the kinds of holiday they had. Report back to the class. Compare and discuss your findings.

RECENT DEVELOPMENTS

Listening

TOURISM TRENDS

1))) **1.3** Monica Cheung works for the Hong Kong Travel Research Centre. Listen to her talking about trends in tourism over the past ten years and complete the summary.

People now book their vacations online and personalize their itineraries. This means that, although the High Street travel agent ¹_____ yet, the retail agent ²_____ fast.

There is a(n) ³_____ towards more sustainable tourism and governments in ⁴_____ countries are attracting inward investment. As a result, remote areas ⁵_____ up, there are more jobs and profits ⁶_____. Adventure tourism and extreme sports are increasingly popular and this segment ⁷_____ rapidly.

Current trends in demography and lifestyle are also important. The number of customized vacations for the seniors market ⁸_____. There is another important ⁹_____ trend associated with increased levels of stress in people's work and daily lives. As a result, there has been a(n) ¹⁰_____ from vacations focused on entertainment towards more spiritual experiences, designed to improve health and wellness.

2))) Listen again. What prediction for the future does Monica Cheung make? Do you agree with her? What other predictions would you make?

GRAMMAR: CONTINUOUS ASPECT

1 Use the **present continuous** to talk about situations that are changing, developing or progressing.
The High Street retail travel agent hasn't disappeared yet but is disappearing.
Governments in emerging countries are trying to attract foreign direct investment.
People are living under increased levels of stress.

2 Use the **present perfect continuous** to describe a situation or activity that started in the past and has been in progress for a period until now.
So, are there any trends that have been emerging over the last ten years or so?
The number of people over 55 has been increasing steadily in Europe.

3 Use the **past continuous** to describe past events repeated over time.
A few years ago people were saying that the future lay in space travel.

4 You can use continuous forms with modal verbs or the passive.
People who go on a round-the-world cruise may be fulfilling a dream.
In emerging countries remote areas are being opened up and jobs are being created.

5 Use continuous forms to indicate that the event or situation is unfinished.
People are increasingly looking for a meaning to their lives.
I don't think that any tourists will be staying on the moon in the foreseeable future.

See Grammar reference, page 111.

3 Study the Grammar box. <u>Underline</u> the verb forms and identify the tenses used in the sentences. In each case, is the situation finished (F) or unfinished (U)?

1 We've seen a complete reversal of the previous trend. F / U

2 We've been selling a large number of adventure holidays. F / U

3 Many old buildings have been destroyed to make way for new office blocks. F / U

4 More and more people are using their smartphones to make bookings. F / U

5 Climate change is having a profound impact on tourism. F / U

6 Residents of India and China are becoming more mobile than ever before. F / U

4 Complete the article with the correct form of the verbs in brackets. There may be more than one possible answer.

A portrait of China

Drawn by the air of mystery, the number of visitors to China ¹_____ (rise) rapidly. The moment they get off the plane, many tourists ²_____ (may / fulfil) a lifelong dream to see a country that for years seemed cut off from the rest of the world.

The Great Wall ³_____ (rebuild) completely in parts but its dizzying loops across the horizon still leave most visitors lost for words. The Forbidden City at the heart of Beijing ⁴_____ (draw) crowds that make its original majesty hard to imagine. But Beijing ⁵_____ (change) dramatically and ⁶_____ (still / change). In recent times the capital ⁷_____ (see) obvious economic development – luxury hotels, convenient public transport, modern shopping malls and excellent restaurants. However, much of the traditional housing ⁸_____ (destroy) to make way for new highways which are choked with traffic, making the air difficult to breathe.

China's vast population, despite famines and civil wars, ⁹_____ (grow) from 400 million to approximately 1.4 billion in less than a century. This increase in population ¹⁰_____ (drive) a seemingly never-ending consumer boom in recent years, most evident in the cities with their stores selling fast food, smartphones and facelifts.

With few opportunities for work in the countryside, millions of people ¹¹_____ (move) to the cities in search of a better life. So if your taxi driver doesn't know where he ¹²_____ (go), it's because he ¹³_____ (also / just / arrive) in town!

Writing

A PORTRAIT OF …

5 In what ways has your country changed in recent times? Write a description (250–280 words) for an airline magazine of the developments that have taken/are taking place. Use the topics in the box and the article in Exercise 4 to help you.

> culture   economy   family life   lifestyle   politics
> population   tourism   working patterns

PROFESSIONAL SKILLS
USING VISUALS

Reading

EUROPEAN TRAVEL TRENDS

1 Read the extract from a report about travel trends in Europe. What are the general trends in the categories below: upward, downward or steady/level?

1 visitor numbers **2** European airlines **3** hotel occupancy

Executive summary: trends for the first semester

The majority of European destinations are indicating a positive start to the year. Foreign visitor arrivals <u>went up</u> <u>steadily</u> during the first six months and the number of days spent in each country is also on the <u>rise</u>.

Both airline and hotel industry data confirm the <u>upward</u> trend in travel to Europe. However, visitor numbers have been <u>growing</u> more <u>gradually</u> than during the peak growth periods of last year.

International passenger traffic <u>outpaced</u> global growth over the first two months of the year. European airlines have also reported a <u>modest</u> <u>increase</u> in traffic over the first 14 weeks but passenger numbers have <u>declined</u> <u>slightly</u> over recent weeks.

The capacity of European airlines continues to <u>expand</u>, carrying on the trend from late last year. Capacity <u>soared</u> between November and March, averaging an 8.8 percent rise in Available Seat Kilometres over the first 14 weeks. This should translate into competitive fares and <u>boost</u> travel demand over the next 6–8 months.

Hotel occupancy has <u>improved</u> <u>further</u> but appears to have <u>levelled off</u>. Average daily rates continue to <u>rise</u> <u>fast</u> across Europe in response to demand. However, overall growth is expected to <u>dip</u> as a result of the <u>sharp</u> <u>hike</u> in energy prices, which is leading to a <u>significant</u> <u>decrease</u> in disposable income and a <u>surge</u> in transportation costs.

2 Complete the table with the <u>underlined</u> words describing trends in the extract in Exercise 1. Change verbs to their infinitive form.

Nouns	Verbs	Adverbs	Adjectives

3 Look at the table in Exercise 2. Which words indicate a rapid or sudden change? Which verb means 'to stop rising or falling'?

Vocabulary

DESCRIBING VISUALS

4 Look at the four different ways of showing statistics. Label the visuals A–D with the words in the box.

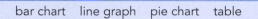

> bar chart   line graph   pie chart   table

A

Tourist arrivals

1 _____

tourist arrivals

France Spain Italy UK

B

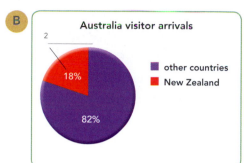

Australia visitor arrivals

2 _____

18%

82%

■ other countries
■ New Zealand

_____

_____

C

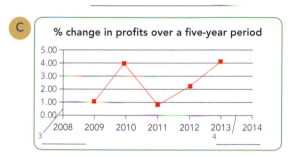

% change in profits over a five-year period

2008 2009 2010 2011 2012 2013 2014

3 _____   4 _____

_____

D

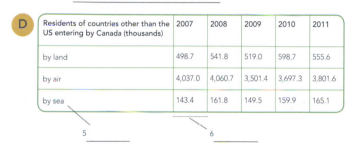

Residents of countries other than the US entering by Canada (thousands)	2007	2008	2009	2010	2011
by land	498.7	541.8	519.0	598.7	555.6
by air	4,037.0	4,060.7	3,501.4	3,697.3	3,801.6
by sea	143.4	161.8	149.5	159.9	165.1

5 _____   6 _____

_____

5 Label the features 1–6 in the visuals in Exercise 4 with the words in the box.

> bar   column   horizontal axis   row   segment   vertical axis

Listening

PRESENTING STATISTICS

6))) 1.4   Listen to part of a talk about using visual aids to present statistics and complete the Professional skills box.

PROFESSIONAL SKILLS: USING VISUALS

Introduction	Topic	Circumstances
This bar chart [1] _____	the number of tourist arrivals	in the world's most visited countries.
The pie chart [2] _____	visitor arrivals	for the period in question.
The red shaded segment [3] _____	the number of visitors from New Zealand	during the first semester.
The line graph [4] _____	the percentage change in profits	over the last few years.
The table gives us a(n) [5] _____	of residents entering Canada	by land, air and sea.

Speaking

DESCRIBING A VISUAL

7 Work in pairs. Student A, turn to file 1, page 102. Student B, turn to file 20, page 108. Take turns to describe your visual for your partner to draw and complete with the correct information. Start by explaining what your visual represents.

RESEARCH

Research some recent statistics relating to tourists visiting your country. If possible, find out about visitor arrivals, their country of origin, hotel occupancy, average length of stay and spending patterns. Present your findings to the class.

CASE STUDY
TAILOR A PACKAGE

CASE STUDY MENU

Aim: To design a package for Chinese tourists.

1 Read an email about the boom in Chinese tourism.
2 Listen to a representative of the China Travel Market Research Institute.
3 Read an email from a tour operator in Beijing.
4 Write a proposal for a suitable package.

Getaway Travel

1 **Diane Sullivan is a senior partner in the Getaway travel agency in London. Read her email to her junior colleagues and answer the questions.**

1 What prediction has the World Tourism Organization (WTO) made?

2 What explains the growth of outbound tourism?

3 What do the numbers 8.3, 6.4% and 17.5% represent?

WTOs

From:	Diane Sullivan
To:	Hannah Williams; Dan Bower; Kevin Jones

The European travel market has levelled off in recent years and may even go into decline, so I think the time is ripe to investigate the Chinese outbound market. I've done some initial spadework and found out the following:

- 66 million Chinese tourists travelled overseas last year – an increase of 8.3 million.
- The WTO reckons China will be the fourth largest international market by 2020, representing 6.4 percent of the total market share.
- The growth of China's outbound tourism, 17.5 percent year–on–year, is much faster than for inbound tourism.

The Chinese economy is still growing and people now have much more disposable income, so I need the team to do some research and generate ideas on how to cater to this emerging market.

Research interviews

2)) 1.5 **Listen to Hannah and Dan from Getaway Travel interviewing an expert on the Chinese outbound market. He identifies two types of tourist: Generation X (older first-time travellers) and Generation Y (mid 20s, highly educated, affluent). Complete the table with information about them.**

	Generation X (1960–1980)	Generation Y (aged 20–30)
travel motivation		
where from in China		
accommodation preferences		
preferred activities and interests on holiday		

An email from Beijing

3 Getaway Travel have received the email below. What is Huang Meng offering? How does he make the offer sound attractive?

From:	Huang.Meng@qùtours.cn
To:	info@getaway.eu
Subject:	China travel

We are an established travel agency in Beijing and are looking for European partners to take advantage of the growing number of Chinese wanting to travel to Europe and elsewhere. Less than five percent of China's over 22,000 travel agencies are engaged in the outbound tourism business and we wish to grow our business in partnership with overseas suppliers such as yourselves.

Could you offer a ten-day tour to famous places for groups of married couples and arrange suitable accommodation and transportation? We also have business delegations who would want to combine sightseeing and cultural trips with their professional duties.

We look forward to hearing from you.

Huang Meng
Chief Executive, Qù Tours

A feedback meeting

4))) 1.6 After the interview Hannah, Dan and Kevin from Getaway Travel get together to compare notes. Listen and complete the fact file.

Chinese visitor fact file
- Food is not a priority. Most European food is ^{1}_____.
- They prize luxury European goods because they are ^{2}_____.
- They enjoy visiting ^{3}_____.
- Semi-FITs need a tour guide who is ^{4}_____.
- Chinese visitors appreciate visitor information in ^{5}_____.
- Most high-spending tourism comes from ^{6}_____.

TASK

5 Work in small groups. In response to Huang Meng's email, decide what kind of ten-day tour you could organize for groups of Chinese visitors to your country.

Decide on:
- the profile of visitor your package is aimed at.
- the type of accommodation you would book.
- the best things for the group to see and do.
- a possible itinerary for the group.

6 Write an email to Huang Meng with a proposal for a ten-day tour that could be marketed by Qù Tours. Give reasons for your choices.

UNIT 1: KEY WORDS

affluent   cater for   charter
consumer boom   current   date back to
demography   FIT   inward investment
level off   outbound/inbound
recharge batteries   segment   surge
vertical/horizontal axis

See DVD-ROM Mini-dictionary

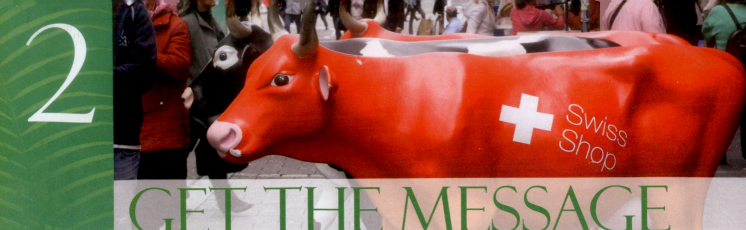

2

GET THE MESSAGE

UNIT MENU

Grammar: countable and uncountable nouns
Vocabulary: advertising and publicity, web words, collocations
Professional skills: maintaining a website
Case study: Genesis Valley – improve a media profile

Vocabulary

ADVERTISING AND PUBLICITY

1 **Look at the dictionary entries. What do [C] and [U] stand for?**

ad·ver·tise·ment n [C]
[əd'vɜːtɪsmənt *BrE*;
ˌædvərˈtaɪzmənt *AmE*]
also **ad** (informal); **advert** *BrE*
a picture, set of words or a short
film intended to persuade
people to buy a product or use
a service
We've taken out a full-page
advertisement in The Times.

pub·lic·i·ty n [U] [pʌbˈlɪsəti]
free content about a person or
a company that appears in the
media
The 'Save the Coastline'
movement has just launched a
new publicity campaign on
Facebook.

ad·ver·tis·ing n [U] [ˈædvətaɪzɪŋ]
content you pay for on TV, in
newspapers, on the web, etc.
They spend millions of dollars
on television advertising.

2 **Are the following advertising (A) or publicity (P)?**

1 a television commercial broadcast during prime time A / P

2 space purchased for a banner embedded in a commercial website A / P

3 a message about an upcoming event posted on Twitter A / P

4 a description of your Caribbean cruise on TripAdvisor A / P

GRAMMAR: COUNTABLE AND UNCOUNTABLE NOUNS

1 Unlike **countable nouns**, **uncountable nouns** are
not used with *a/an* and do not have a plural form.
advice (NOT *an advice* or *advices*)
advertising (NOT *an advertising* or *advertisings*)

2 Some nouns have countable or uncountable uses.
The internet grew incredibly fast over a very short
space *of time.* (C)

A Twitter message only gives you ***space*** *for up to*
140 characters. (U)

A good working ***knowledge*** *of programming*
languages would be an asset. (C)

Most people have very little ***knowledge*** *of how*
the internet works. (U)

See Grammar reference, pages 111 and 112.

3 **Study the Grammar box. Then use a dictionary to check the meanings and uses of**
the words in the box. Which of them are never used with *a/an* or in the plural?

copy   design   feedback   hype   information   investment   promotion   travel

4 **Complete the pairs of sentences with the correct form of a word from the box in Exercise 3. Are the words countable (C) or uncountable (U)?**

1 a I want a job with good prospects for _____. C / U

   b We're doing a special winter sports _____. C / U

2 a We're looking at a new _____ for the company logo. C / U

   b She did a course in web _____ during her third year at college. C / U

3 a The tax cuts are aimed at stimulating _____ in tourism. C / U

   b She's made a huge _____ in time and effort to get this done. C / U

4 a I'm very happy with the _____ for the new full-page advertisement. C / U

   b Could you give me a(n) _____ of last year's financial report? C / U

5 a They say that _____ broadens the mind but I'm not sure it does. C / U

   b She's off on her _____ again and won't be back for another six months. C / U

Vocabulary

WEB WORDS

5 **Match the words 1–10 with the definitions a–j.**

1	link	**a**	the first page of a website
2	font	**b**	a list of choices which appears on a computer screen
3	bandwidth	**c**	move information up or down on a screen
4	crash	**d**	the way text and images are set out on a page
5	cursor	**e**	a connection from a word or image on a webpage to another webpage
6	layout	**f**	transfer a program or webpage from a remote server to a computer
7	menu	**g**	the amount of data that can be transmitted at one time
8	home page	**h**	a moving mark or arrow to navigate around a computer screen
9	scroll	**i**	the size and style of text displayed on a computer screen
10	load	**j**	stop working completely

Listening

A NEW WEBSITE

6 **))) 2.1** **Listen to Brad and Kristin trying out their new website and circle the correct options in italics.**

1 The website is taking a long time to *load / shut down / refresh*.

2 Kristin thinks that they don't have enough *bytes / bandwidth / images*.

3 The *graphics / headers / links* are all in different colours.

4 There *is too much text / are too many pictures / are too many videos* on the site.

5 The video *opens up in Internet Explorer / opens in a new window / won't open*.

Writing

BRIEFING A WEB DESIGNER

7 **Work in pairs. Student A, turn to file 2, page 102. Student B, turn to file 21, page 108. Share the information and put the features in order of importance. Then write a set of instructions for a new designer. Include the points below.**

- the information on the home page
- the number of pages on the site and their content
- your ideas on layout (menus, images, etc.)
- the design features you consider important

SOCIAL MEDIA

Speaking

SOCIAL MEDIA

1 **Work in pairs. Discuss the questions with a partner.**

   1 Do you use social media? Which services do you use and what do you use them for?

   2 How can a travel organization promote a destination through social media?

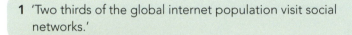

2 **Work with a different partner. Read what different people are saying about social media. Exchange information with your partner and make a list of the advantages and disadvantages of using social media in tourism promotion. Are the benefits stronger than the disadvantages? Student A, look at the information below. Student B, turn to file 3, page 102.**

> **1** 'Two thirds of the global internet population visit social networks.'

> **2** 'People are abandoning email in favour of social media.'

> **3** 'It's great for responding to negative feedback on travel review sites like TripAdvisor or Travbuddy.'

> **4** 'Businesses can foster communication between their customers without trying to manage their conversations.'

> **5** 'It doesn't require huge financial investment – your customers do the work for you.'

> **6** 'The positive word of mouse message is more credible than traditional advertising.'

> **7** 'Social networks are "viral". A video or tweet can be seen by millions within hours.'

Reading

ISLANDREEFJOB.COM

3 **You are going to read an article about a social media campaign to promote the Great Barrier Reef in Australia. Write three questions about things you would like to know about the campaign. Share your questions with a partner.**

4 **Read the article on page 19. Does it answer any of your questions from Exercise 3?**

5 **Read the article again and answer the questions.**

   1 How did candidates apply for the job?

   2 How was the best candidate selected?

   3 To what extent was this campaign innovative and traditional?

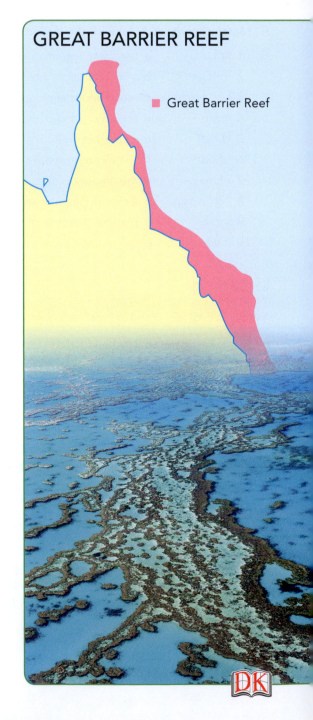

GREAT BARRIER REEF

■ Great Barrier Reef

DK

The best job in the world

A few years ago Tourism Queensland set aside $1.2 million for a groundbreaking social media campaign, targeted at 'global experience seekers', to promote the Great Barrier Reef. The campaign was launched as *The best job in the world* and invited applications for a caretaker to live on the islands of the Great Barrier Reef and report back to the world via weekly blogs, a photo diary, video updates and ongoing media interviews.

To apply for the job, candidates had to record a 60-second video application demonstrating their creativity, suitability, knowledge of the region and enthusiasm for the role. The videos were uploaded to the islandreefjob.com website and hosted through YouTube. People who watched voted on the videos, thereby focusing on the quality of the posts and not just the volume of traffic.

At each stage of the campaign the website was refreshed with new content, emails were sent to site subscribers informing them of developments, and social networking sites were constantly updated. Individual applicants created their own blogs and podcasts, and generally spread the message through 'word of mouse'. Simultaneously, the campaign director organized offline public relations by generating media coverage, classified ads, banner advertising, photography on Flickr and job listings strategically placed in key markets.

Vocabulary

COLLOCATIONS

6 **Match the nouns in the box from the article with the groups of verbs 1–5.**

> a campaign   candidates   money   a video   a website

1 waste/set aside/spend _____

2 shortlist/interview/select _____

3 record/upload/host _____

4 launch/run/mount _____

5 refresh/update/host _____

Listening

THE BEST JOB IN THE WORLD

7))) 2.2 **Listen to an interview with Mark Scholl, who was involved in evaluating the famous *The best job in the world* campaign. Tick (✓) the statements he agrees with.**

1 ___ Conventional advertising is dead.

2 ___ It's impossible to measure the success of a campaign like this.

3 ___ Social media doesn't lead to true dialogue.

4 ___ The initial budget was barely adequate for its purpose.

5 ___ The return on investment was rather disappointing.

8))) **Listen again. What do these numbers represent? Look at audio script 2.2 on page 117 and check your answers. Then practise saying the numbers.**

1 475,000 _____

2 $165,000,000 _____

3 3,000,000,000 _____

4 34,684 _____

5 53,889,455 _____

6 8.62 _____

PROFESSIONAL SKILLS
MAINTAINING A WEBSITE

Listening

GENERATING WEBSITE TRAFFIC

1 How can a web designer generate traffic to a website? Discuss with a partner.

2))) **2.3** Listen to a presentation by Kevin, a webmaster, on how to maintain and improve a travel website and complete the Professional skills box. Use no more than FIVE words in each gap.

PROFESSIONAL SKILLS: MAINTAINING AND IMPROVING A WEBSITE

1 Make your site attractive and add new content [1]_____. Don't let it go stale.

2 Attract attention to your site by posting regular [2]_____. Create a menu for new posts which will be recognized as [3]_____ by search engines.

3 Ask visitors to [4]_____, published at regular intervals. Preferably, the content should be customized to a specific audience. Send your customers an email with a link for them to click on.

4 Provide links to podcasts, which are an excellent way of broadcasting information, especially when delivered through [5]_____.

5 Use [6]_____ on your website as it is the [7]_____ to capture the attraction of your destination in sound and movement.

6 Optimize your site to enable [8]_____ to rank your site high on the list. Use meaningful headers with meta tags which the search engines will identify as relevant.

3 Kevin has also created a blog in which he gives advice to web designers on improving website traffic. Read the extract from his blog and circle the correct options in italics.

What a search engine does is to [1]*report / scan / notice* your website based on the number of [2]*hits / loads / media*, the number of links and the frequency of changes you make to it. This means that if you're not constantly [3]*updating / drafting / broadcasting* your site and adding content, the search robots may not visit your site very frequently and your search [4]*range / analysis / ranking* will fall. So the more frequently you add content, the more visible your site will be. Here are some suggestions regarding how often you should make any new posts:

- **News releases:** as a rule of thumb, one to four a month is appropriate.
- **Newsletters:** once a month is normal; quarterly or even six to eight times a year is acceptable.

- **Podcasts:** their frequency can vary greatly but try to [5]*spread / distribute / broadcast* them on a regular basis and follow up from time to time as appropriate.
- [6]*Screened / Embedded / Generated* **videos:** depending on your content, you could be posting videos weekly or monthly. There are no hard and fast rules here but the more, the better.
- **Profiles and interviews:** maybe twice a week for a period of intense web [7]*traffic / circulation / coverage* (in high season, for example) or, as an ongoing strategy, on a monthly basis.

In my experience, the more you create, the more there is to create. When web content is constantly on your mind, you are always thinking of new and creative ways to use the web to communicate.

Writing

UPDATING TERMS AND CONDITIONS

4 As the webmaster for your company's site, you have received the email below from your boss about some changes that need to be made to the information about deposits and final payments. Rewrite the paragraph below making the ten changes.

From: Matt Simmonds

To: Webmaster

The information below on the website is inaccurate or incomplete. I have cut and pasted it from the website and need you to incorporate new text. Could you please do this and get back to me by tomorrow morning? Thanks.

1　The deposit cannot be transferred (not refunded).

2　Say that each person has to pay this sum individually.

3　Add that they will then get an invoice to confirm the reservation (but state how).

4　We don't accept money orders any more.

5　Add the time limit here (say that the date the deposit falls due is stated on the booking form).

6　This doesn't apply to all departures.

7　We need to add here that when we receive their money, it means that they agree to the terms and conditions.

8　OK, but state how. It can't be over the phone as there wouldn't be a written trace.

9　Write something to the effect that if there are mistakes on the invoice, we reserve the right to send out another one and this time with the right price on it.

10　And that means that we get to keep their deposit!

Deposits and final payments

A [1]non-refundable deposit of $350 per [2]vacation is required for Cygnus Tours to reserve space on your chosen tour. Your booking is not confirmed and payment is not deemed made until the deposit is received by Cygnus. [3] Cygnus accepts cheques, [4]money orders, Visa, MasterCard and American Express. Your reservation will be automatically cancelled if your deposit is not received by Cygnus. [5] [6] Deposits may be required at the time of booking to hold or confirm space for you. [7] Please check your booking invoice and contact Cygnus immediately if your invoice appears to be incorrect, as it may be impossible to make changes later. Cygnus cannot accept responsibility if we are not notified [8] of inaccuracies within seven days of sending out the invoice. [9] Final payment is due 45 days prior to departure. If final payment is not received by the due date, your reservation will be cancelled. [10]

e.g. A [1]*non-transferrable* deposit of $350

21

CASE STUDY
IMPROVE A MEDIA PROFILE

CASE STUDY MENU

Aim: To improve the media profile of a tourist attraction.

1 Read about the Genesis Valley project.
2 Listen to some problems concerning the Genesis Valley centre.
3 Read a media consultant's report.
4 Prepare an action plan to improve the centre's media profile.

The Genesis Valley project

1 **Read the extract from the Genesis Valley project home page and the article that follows and answer the questions.**

   1 What kind of visitor is likely to be attracted to Genesis Valley?

   2 How successful is the Genesis Valley project?

   3 What are the possible reasons for its popularity or lack of popularity?

The Genesis Valley project

The Genesis Valley project began life ten years ago as a regional tourism initiative to attract visitors to a post-industrial mining valley. After the pits were closed, the area was restored to nature, trees were planted and work began on creating 1,000 hectares of parkland.

Genesis Valley now hosts a number of attractions: a Museum of Mankind, a zoo and aquarium, an amusement park, a snake house and insectarium, a tropical greenhouse and ornamental gardens. It is owned by the Genesis Foundation, a group of anthropologists, earth scientists and horticulturalists and is managed as a private limited company.

How to reach us
Take the M7 motorway as far as Chilling Cross and then follow the signs to Abbots Bickington and Stanston (B256). Before you get to Stanston, take a sharp right and continue for about two miles. Turn left at the crossroads and drive down into the valley. The entrance is opposite the Garden Centre.

Genesis project on the rocks

Genesis Valley has just celebrated its tenth anniversary but there is little cause for celebration. Despite encouraging visitor numbers when first launched in a blaze of national publicity, the crowds that thronged the entrance turnstiles a decade ago have been growing thinner and thinner. A number of reasons for the plunging popularity of Genesis Valley have been put forward: unpredictable weather, a reduction in disposable income, even changing patterns in the leisure interests of children, who seem to be more interested in surfing the web and playing online video games than enjoying a day out with Mum and Dad. Whatever the reasons, the management will need to come up with some new ideas and make them happen if Genesis Valley is not to go into irremediable decline.

Communication failure

2))) **2.4** **Listen and match the conversations 1–4 with the contexts a–d.**

a a tour guide talking to a group of visitors ___   **c** visitors driving to Genesis Valley ___

b a meeting to discuss a website ___   **d** visitors inside Genesis Valley ___

3))) **All the conversations illustrate how Genesis Valley is failing to communicate with and satisfy its customers. Listen again and answer the questions.**

1 What problems or shortcomings does each conversation illustrate?

2 How could these problems be solved?

A consultant's report

4 **Genesis Valley has asked a media consultant for help with attracting more visitors. Read the extracts from her report. Which ideas do you think are the most useful?**

One idea would be to take a photo of each visitor or family entering the attraction, for them to buy at a modest price. This would generate revenue and be a souvenir of an enjoyable day out. If the photo contained the name *Genesis Valley*, postal address, web URL and phone number, the real advertising payoff would occur when that photo was uploaded for the world to see.

Certain staff members need training in presenting to the public and/or are lacking in people skills. Some visitors I interviewed said the staff were rude to their children. Unfortunately, one regrettable incident can then be described on a site such as TripAdvisor and create a damaging impression. On the other hand, it takes just one inspired employee to say, 'I hope you had a great stay, please write a nice review and tell your friends.'

TASK

5 **Work in pairs. Look at the memo from the Genesis Valley managing director and the bar chart and prepare for the meeting. Find two or three ideas for each of the points in the memo.**

From: Sally McGowan
To: Marketing task force

The next meeting is to discuss our promotional strategy and how to boost visitor numbers. Please come prepared with ideas concerning:

- the percentage breakdown of money spent on advertising.
- the suggestions put forward by the media consultant.
- revamping our website (new content and design).
- how to fish where the fish are: understanding our clientele and making our messages more relevant to them.
- using social media to maintain interest among existing customers and attract new ones.

We need to work within a budget of £20,000 and implement our ideas within the next three months.

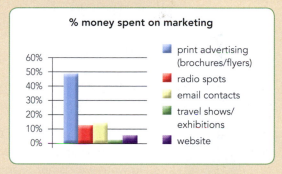

6 **Work in groups of four. Roleplay the meeting. Discuss all your ideas and agree on an action plan for how to attract more visitors to Genesis Valley and turn it into a popular attraction. Then present your plan to the class.**

3

HOTEL BRANDING

UNIT MENU

Grammar: making predictions
Vocabulary: brands
Professional skills: creating a business plan
Case study: the winners – invest in a hotel

Speaking

INTERNATIONAL BRANDS

1 **Work in pairs. Add to the lists of famous international brands.**

    1 Food and drink: Danone, Kellogg's, Pepsi Cola

    2 Clothes and accessories: Gap, Armani, Rolex

    3 Cars: Rolls-Royce, Nissan, Peugeot

    4 Technology: Apple, Samsung, Siemens

2 **Why do people buy these brands? What thoughts, emotions and values do the brand names communicate? Discuss with your partner. Refer to the words in the box.**

> family life   fashion   fitness   glamour   health   innovation   luxury   reliability
> safety   style   success   value for money   wealth   youth

Listening

BRANDING IN THE HOSPITALITY INDUSTRY

3))) 3.1 **Listen to Part One of a seminar conducted by a lecturer in Hospitality and Marketing at a British university. How does she distinguish a product from a brand? In what way is her example a good illustration of a brand?**

4))) **Listen again and complete the definitions.**

    1 A product is a(n) ¹_____ or a(n) ²_____ that ³_____ in some way.

    2 A brand is a(n) ⁴_____ which ⁵_____ and makes a product or service ⁶_____.

    3 The McDonald's brand is a(n) ⁷_____ involving family, ⁸_____, ⁹_____ and consistently ¹⁰_____.

5))) 3.2 **Listen to Part Two and answer the questions.**

    1 How can a hotel distinguish itself from another hotel in the same price range?

    2 How do large hotel organizations cater to different needs and expectations?

    3 What words describe these features?

       • The name of the hotel is easily recognized.

       • Guests know exactly what to expect.

       • Guests will keep coming back.

Reading

BOUTIQUE HOTELS

6 Work in pairs. Think of the names of some famous hotel chains. What brand values are associated with them?

7 Read the blog post about boutique hotels and answer the questions.

  1 What does the author think was the problem with branded hotels?

  2 List FIVE adjectives in the text that describe a boutique hotel.

  3 In what way(s) are Edition hotels a new departure?

The late 20th century was the age of uninspiring branded hotels, lacking in warmth and personality. A hotel room in Manchester was identical to one in Manila; the bed, the wardrobe, the writing desk all looked the same. Indeed, the Hilton or Holiday Inn brand names were accused of replacing a distinctive sense of place with a bland consistency of design. Independent hoteliers and entrepreneurs therefore began to think outside the box and to develop a more innovative and aesthetically pleasing environment to give guests a more stimulating experience.

The boutique hotel concept is usually attributed to Ian Schrager, who launched the Morgans Hotel on Madison Avenue, New York, in 1984. Here, affordable luxury was offered in a stylish and sophisticated environment, known as 'cheap chic'. Boutique hotels differ from branded hotels by offering a more elegant, intimate setting and a more attentive staff. Many boutique hotels introduce different themes into each guest room, making each stay unique. For example, the Library Hotel in New York City contains over 6,000 volumes for guests to browse. Each floor is dedicated to a different theme, ranging from Maths to New

Media, and the 60 rooms are furnished with books and works of art.

Recently, Bill Marriott Jr., Marriott's CEO, and Mr. Schrager have joined forces and inaugurated a new independent hotel brand called 'Edition', demonstrating that autonomous hoteliers and major brands can work together. Edition hotels aim to provide a one-of-a-kind guest environment which, according to Mr. Schrager, will create 'a new genre, the next phase in the story of lifestyle hotels. We would call it boutique if everybody else wasn't calling their hotels boutique.'

8 Complete the sentences with words formed from the words in capitals.

  1 The hotel had no distinguishing features at all – it was totally _____. INSPIRE

  2 The restaurant has a very cosy and _____ atmosphere. INTIMACY

  3 I found the personnel _____ and always ready to look after my needs. ATTEND

  4 The furniture was both _____ attractive and functional. AESTHETICS

  5 I believe the hotel won an award for its _____ design. INNOVATE

  6 The hotel is immaculate, comfortable and _____,with stunning sea views. STYLE

9 Work in pairs. Discuss your own ideas for a themed boutique hotel in your town or city. Think about the elements below. Present your ideas to the class.

- target market: age group, background, interests
- market sector: luxury, economy, mid-range
- theme: how you would transmit the theme in terms of features, furniture, fittings and décor
- brand values: what emotions, thoughts and values you want your brand to evoke

RESEARCH

Choose a major hotel corporation (e.g. Hyatt, Choice Hotels). Type the name and the word *brands* into a search engine and find out about their different brands and the market segments they cater to. Present your findings to the class.

HOTELS OF THE FUTURE

Listening

THE HOTEL OF THE FUTURE

1 **A well-known hotel chain asked people to tweet their ideas of what the hotel of the future might be like and what facilities it might offer. Read the list of ideas and put them in your order of preference. Then compare your ideas with a partner.**

1 ___ an underwater hotel with a view of the marine life from the windows

2 ___ rooms with a 'dream machine' to control what you dream about

3 ___ 'hotel in the heavens': a zero-gravity orbital hotel located in space

4 ___ a miniature hotel for children with mini furniture

5 ___ each bedroom with its own robot for cleaning and other services

6 ___ a hotel built as pods that can be moved to a new location whenever a guest wants

7 ___ a touch screen wall that converts to a window at the flick of a switch

8 ___ a holographic virtual personal assistant (a menu of caricatures to choose from)

2 **))) 3.3** **Listen to five people talking about future technological developments in hotel rooms. Match the speakers 1–5 with the things they talk about a–e.**

Who talks about:

a the ceiling? ___   **d** the bed? ___

b the window? ___   **e** the shape of the room? __

c the bathroom? ___

GRAMMAR: **MAKING PREDICTIONS**

In English there are many words and expressions for talking about the future, which express different degrees of certainty:

- almost certain: *be bound to, will*
- very possible: *chances are, be highly likely (to), may well, in all likelihood, in all probability*
- possible: *may, might, could, be likely (to)*
- not very probable: *be unlikely (to), probably won't*

See Grammar reference, page 112.

---

3 **)))** **Study the Grammar box. Then listen again and complete the phrases the speakers use to make predictions.**

1 But in the very near future [1]_____ that the design of a typical hotel room will be very different.

2 [2]_____, there'll be a voice-activated computer on the wall …

3 I think that for the next generation of guests it's [3]_____ that they'll be able to choose the décor of the room from a whole rainbow of colours …

4 … you [4]_____ need to switch on the light because the light [5]_____ come on for you. … there's [6]_____ a jacuzzi and there [7]_____ a television for you to watch as you lie back and soak.

5 … once you've checked into the hotel, you [8]_____ want to check out!

Reading

TOMORROW'S GUEST

4 **Read the results of a survey about future developments in the hotel industry and tick (✓) the topics that are mentioned.**

1 ___ business collaboration
2 ___ check-in and departure
3 ___ hotel décor
4 ___ the grey market
5 ___ smartphone booking
6 ___ catering for disability
7 ___ social networks

Catering for the guests of the future

Tomorrow's guest is increasingly likely to demand intense personalization. 92 percent of the people who took part in the survey expressed a wish to have their stay customized according to their needs. These needs will encompass check-in and departure, the size of the rooms, décor and furnishings, audio-visual facilities, and food and beverage options. As a result, two adjacent bedrooms might have individual layouts, different artwork on the walls, one might be minimalist, whereas the other could be equipped with the latest state-of-the-art technology and sophisticated products.

Hotels may well bring in branded products for amenities, bedding and furniture or brand the hotels themselves. One likely development is the association of hotel brands with other brands such as Armani to create a differentiated offering in the marketplace.

96 percent predicted that within the next ten years, hotels will definitely need to develop strong social media 'listening skills' to understand how customer needs and perceptions of brands and service quality are evolving. Marketing messages and pricing will have to reflect the needs of an increasingly diverse customer base. Secure social media could be used to build up a deep profile of an individual that is then used to personalize and enrich the guest experience. Via such networks, hotels will continue to learn about the guest throughout the stay and better match the service to the guest profile in subsequent stays.

One of the most persistent trends hotels will certainly need to address is the changing age profile of society. However, it is unlikely that tomorrow's 60-year-olds will be the same as yesterday's older generation. This implies catering not only for an older traveller but also broader family groupings. In the survey 57 percent said that multigenerational holidays are sure to become increasingly popular.

5 Read the text in Exercise 4 again and <u>underline</u> all the expressions for making predictions. Add any new ones to the list in the Grammar box.

6 Which of the predictions in the text do you think is the most important and has the most immediate implications for hotels today? Discuss with a partner.

RESEARCH

Type words such as *hotel*, *design* and *technology* into a search engine and find out about recent and future developments in how hotels cater to their guests. Report your findings to the class.

PROFESSIONAL SKILLS
CREATING A BUSINESS PLAN

Speaking

STARTING A BUSINESS

1 Work in pairs. Discuss the importance of the items in the box when setting up a business. Why are they important? What would happen if you didn't have them?

> accountant   advertising and marketing plan   business plan   financial advisor
> insurance   market research data   seed capital

2 Complete the Professional skills box. Match the descriptions of the different sections of a business plan 1–7 with the headings a–g.

PROFESSIONAL SKILLS: CREATING A BUSINESS PLAN

1 ___
The plan should open with a concise overview describing your business idea. It condenses the key points you will be making and prepares the reader for what comes next.

2 ___
Detailed CVs and an organization chart can appear in an appendix but your plan should include a description of key personnel, their roles, experience and expertise.

3 ___
This section explains the choice of geographical situation and describes the property and premises.

4 ___
State who your hotel will cater for and define your niche – attracting a budget-conscious traveller is significantly different from appealing to a business traveller or a honeymooning couple.

5 ___
What are your proposals for advertising and public relations? How will future guests be able to find out about you and make a reservation?

6 ___
Outline the risks and rewards in terms of the strengths, weaknesses, opportunities and threats to your venture.

7 ___
The bottom line is what investors will look at first, so make sure you outline your fixed and variable costs and include a balance sheet for the first year's activity.

a Location
b Executive summary
c Financial forecasts
d Management team
e Target clientele
f SWOT analysis
g Marketing plan

---

3 Read these extracts from a business plan and decide which section from Exercise 2 they belong to. Write the headings in A–B below. Then complete the extracts with the words in the boxes.

> balance sheet   break even   earmark   investment

A
_____

For the first year we will ¹_____ a sizeable proportion of income for promotion via accommodation booking websites, brochure advertising and leaflets at tourist attractions in the region. We expect to cover the initial expenditure on advertising during the first three months but will continue to make a substantial ²_____ in promoting the business to ensure first-time and repeat visitors. We believe that our financial projections are realistic and, as you can see from the enclosed ³_____, we believe we can ⁴_____ after nine months of operation.

> advantage   calibre   data   value

B
_____

There are hotels and bed and breakfasts in the region but market research ⁵_____ suggests that the competition does not offer the same ⁶_____ for money. Informal reports indicate that some establishments have failed to attract personnel of the highest ⁷_____. However, if the quality of their service improves, our competitive ⁸_____ could disappear and potential guests may also prefer a location nearer public transport.

Listening

FINANCING A BED AND BREAKFAST

4))) **3.4**   Michael and Sally Gamble are thinking of opening a bed and breakfast. Listen to Part One of their conversation with a financial advisor and complete 1–7 in the table. Then make the calculations and complete A–D.

Project start-up expenses				
Item	Expected cost	Expected life	Annual cost	Monthly overhead
electricity, plumbing, painting, landscaping	$¹_____	10 years	$A_____	$185
bedding (mattresses, sheets, blankets, etc.)	$²_____	³_____	$900	$75
kitchen equipment	$1,200	10 years	$120	$10
road signs and front entrance sign	$⁴_____	5 years	$B_____	$33.33
legal fees	$⁵_____	one-off	$C_____	$D_____
advertising and promotion	$2,400	⁶_____	$2,400	$200
supplies	$600	6 months	$1,200	$100
Total start-up costs	$⁷_____			

5))) **3.5**   Michael and Sally are not sure what to charge as room rates. Listen to the advice they are given in Part Two of the conversation and calculate possible room rates.

Worst-case scenario
- start-up costs: $¹_____ + desired return on investment = $²_____
- target sales revenue: $60,000 ÷ ³_____ bed nights sold = room rate of $⁴_____

Better-case scenario
- start-up costs: $⁵_____ + desired return on investment = $⁶_____
- target sales revenue: $60,000 ÷ ⁷_____ bed nights sold = room rate of $⁸_____

3

CASE STUDY
INVEST IN A HOTEL

CASE STUDY MENU

Aim: To select a hotel to invest in and write a business plan for the project.

1 Read about a group of young prize winners.
2 Compare three potential investments.
3 Listen to a conversation and discuss the advantages and disadvantages of each investment.
4 Write a business plan for the investment of your choice.

Reading

1 **Read the extract from a local newspaper and answer the questions.**

1 What is the good news?
2 What do Teresa and her friends plan to do?

Local students win $3m backing

Three tourism management students have won the backing of several wealthy investors to start their own business. Appearing on the popular television programme *The Business Pitch*, in which budding young entrepreneurs present their start-up ideas to a panel of millionaires with spare cash to donate to worthy projects, the three friends said they were 'over the moon'. 'We'd been looking into the idea of opening up a hotel or guesthouse for a long time and I felt sure we would get their support,' said Teresa Bower, who is in her final year. 'We've learnt all the management skills, so all we need to do now is choose the right property to invest the money in.'

2 **Teresa and her friends, Dave and Sarah, have short-listed three properties they are interested in. Read the descriptions and answer the questions.**

Which property:

1 is the most isolated?
2 has an established clientele?
3 is the most healthy?
4 does not have a fixed selling price?
5 allows for expansion?
6 could attract a corporate clientele?
7 enables the owners to live on site?

Waterfront Hotel, Saaremaa Island, Estonia   ~~150,0000~~

The largest island in Estonia, Saaremaa, is the jewel of its archipelago. There are many things to see and do but its extraordinary natural beauty is the reason why so many people feel compelled to return to the region.

This 120-year old guesthouse overlooks a river with the best freshwater fishing in the country. There is unlimited parking for guests and plenty of room for adding other amenities. Many rooms have been renovated and furnished with antiques. Each guest room has cable television, air conditioning, telephone and private bath. There is no competition as this is the only accommodation in the region.

Asking price: $3,165,000   115,000

Black Hills Motel, South Dakota

This franchised motel is close to all major tourist attractions and is an ideal location for small weddings, family reunions and business retreats. Many of the guests are regular customers. All 16 guest rooms are equipped with an air purification system designed to reduce allergies and kill 99 percent of all known germs but some rooms need refurbishing. The owners have a private residential suite and qualify for owner-occupied tax status.

Asking price: $3,250,000
Franchise fee: $45,000
On-going royalty: 6%
General manager training: 3 days
On-going support: toll-free phone line, shared reservation system, grand opening, security/safety procedures
Marketing: free newsletter, national and regional advertising

Boutique Hotel, Mallorca

Situated in one of the loveliest spots on the island of Mallorca, approximately 20 minutes from Palma, this is a rare opportunity for anyone who wishes to move to a warm Mediterranean island and work eight months a year as the independent owner of a prestigious boutique hotel.

The rooms are individually decorated, the common theme

being rustic sophistication, with bright floral fabrics, beamed ceilings and marble tiles.

Aromatic flowers and plants are abundant in the garden.

Asking price: Negotiable. Seven years ago the property cost $2.8 million. Another $300,000 was invested in improvements. Four years ago the property was valued at $3.7 million. Now the market has fallen steeply and we will accept any reasonable offer.

Speaking

3 Which of the hotels do you prefer? Why? Discuss with a partner.

Listening

4))) 3.6 The three friends have done some extra research and are discussing the revenue each property is likely to generate. Listen and complete the table.

Hotel	Occupancy, high season	Occupancy, low season	Room rate, high season	Room rate, low season	Turnover	Profit per annum
Black Hills Motel, South Dakota	90%	^{1}___%	$^{2}___	$^{3}___	$406,000	$^{4}___
Waterfront Hotel, Estonia	^{5}___%	^{6}___%	$175	$^{7}___	$420,000	$^{8}___
Boutique Hotel, Mallorca	^{9}___%	n/a	$^{10}___	n/a	$^{11}___	$90,000–100,00

TASK

5 As the prize money does not cover the full purchase cost of the hotel, a bank loan is necessary. Write a business plan for the hotel of your choice to send to the bank to support your request. Use the section headings from the Professional skills box on page 28 and add any information you think necessary.

UNIT 3: KEY WORDS

affordable   balance sheet   clientele
comply with   earmark   fixtures
franchised   occupancy   overhead
overlook   permit (n)   refurbishment
renovate   royalty   start-up

See DVD-ROM Mini dictionary

31

4

SUSTAINABILITY

Listening

TOURISM IN GOA

1 What are the possible positive and negative effects of a sudden rapid growth of tourism in a developing nation or region such as Goa? Discuss with a partner.

Location:	western coastal region of India, smallest state covering an area of 3,702 sq km
Population:	approximately 1.4 million
Capital:	Panaji
Largest city:	Vasco
Climate:	temperate (average 25–30°C), except during the June–September monsoon season
Tourism:	high season: November–March

Annual tourist numbers in Goa (domestic and international)

3,000,000					2,644,805
2,500,000				2,302,146	
2,000,000					
1,500,000		1,107,705			
1,000,000	881,323		1,268,513		
5,000	775,212				
	1985 1990 1995 2000 2005 2010				

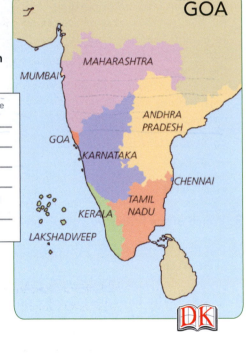

GOA

MAHARASHTRA

MUMBAI

ANDHRA PRADESH

GOA

KARNATAKA

CHENNAI

TAMIL NADU

KERALA

LAKSHADWEEP

DK

2))) **4.1** Listen to four people who work in tourism in Goa talking about how the industry has affected them. Match the speakers 1–4 with the things they say a–g.

Who:

a works part-time in Goa? ___

b is exploited by an employer? ___

c enjoys mixing with foreign tourists? ___

d is involved in a new development? ___

e has to work long hours? ___

f may be a victim of a local government decision? ___

g feels that tourism has not benefited local people? ___

Reading

IMPACTS OF TOURISM GROWTH

3 Read the article on developments in tourism in Goa and list the environmental, social and economic problems.

Goa: Paradise Lost

In the 1980s the former Portuguese colony of Goa became a favourite destination for hippies and backpackers attracted to its natural beauty and relaxed lifestyle. Their impact on Goa was minimal as they adapted to the local way of life, eating local food and living in simple rented accommodation. They provided extra income to traditional communities and often made long-lasting friendships.

Since then Goa has become a money-spinner for specialist and mass market operators and although the government initially welcomed this influx, the negative impacts in recent years have outweighed the positive.

Environmental impacts: While tourists splash in the swimming pools, locals have to put up with water shortages with fatal consequences on Goan agriculture. Hotels consume vast amounts of building materials and electricity, and create a great deal of waste. The absence of efficient public transport has substantially increased the number of motorbikes and cars, which has aggravated environmental pollution.

Social impacts: Many young Goans are losing their sense of culture and identity, and replacing it with a hedonistic culture similar to that found in parts of Ibiza, Greece or Spain. With mass tourism also comes increased crime. The coasts are being bought up by overseas investors and the beach shacks, bars and restaurants have become centres of mafia activity. The tourism industry has been accused of covering up things such as money laundering and people trafficking.

Economic impacts: The benefits to the host community have been minimal as most of the profits line the pockets of external stakeholders, the foreign investors who create the infrastructure to meet Western tourists' demands. This leakage means that very little profit has accrued to local people. When the locals do succeed in profiting from tourism, it is the privileged commercial groups that benefit, not those who suffer the negative consequences.

65 percent of rented properties are owned by non-resident Goans, 20–25 percent by Goans from India's cities and 10–15 percent by natives from Goa. Large hotels and external providers are reaping the economic rewards, while the local population has to bear the social and environmental burden. Potential profits are also being siphoned off by neighbouring states as Goa imports food products from Karnataka and Maharashtra instead of supporting local farmers.

Vocabulary

TOURISM AND COMMUNITY

4 Complete the sentences with the words in the box.

> host community   infrastructure   leakage
> sourcing   stakeholder

1 Anyone who is a potential _____ should be involved in sustainable tourism.
2 A study of _____ in Thailand estimated that 70 percent of tourism revenue ended up leaving the country.
3 The cultural impact of tourism on the _____ has not been properly evaluated.
4 Without a decent _____ – airports, road networks, hotels, etc. – poorer nations cannot attract tourists without foreign investment.
5 _____ goods and supplies locally is more economical than importing them.

Writing

GOA: A MORE SUSTAINABLE FUTURE

5 Work in Pairs. Student A, turn to file 4, page 102. Student B, turn to file 11, page 105. Read the ideas about making tourism in Goa more sustainable. Share the information with your partner and draw up a list of proposals for the future divided into social, economic and environmental categories. Then write a report (450 words) for the Goa Responsible Tourism Association describing the measures that could minimize the negative impacts. Include social, economic and environmental issues. Use the model in the Writing bank on page 96 to help you.

RESEARCH

Use the internet to find out about the current impacts of tourism in another part of the world and suggest ways in which sustainable tourism can be organized to benefit the host community more effectively.

THE GALAPAGOS

Reading

THE GALAPAGOS

1 What do you know about the Galapagos islands? Do the quiz and find out.

2))) 4.2   Listen to the Galapagos Tourist Information Centre audio guide and check your answers in Exercise 1.

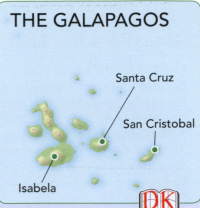

THE GALAPAGOS

Santa Cruz

San Cristobal

Isabela

DK

The Galapagos quiz

1 Which person is associated with the Galapagos Islands?
  a Christopher Columbus **b** Hernán Cortés **c** Marco Polo **d** Charles Darwin

2 Which country do the islands belong to?
  a England **b** Ecuador **c** Argentina **d** South Africa

3 In which ocean are they situated?
  a the Pacific Ocean **b** the Atlantic Ocean **c** the Indian Ocean **d** the Southern (Antarctic) Ocean

4 How many people live on the islands?
  a about 40,000 **b** about 65,000 **c** about 100,000 **d** more than 100,000

5 How many tourists visit the islands every year?
  a about 40,000 **b** about 50,000 **c** about 120,000 **d** about 160,000

6 The Galapagos penguin is the only species of penguin to live on the equator. True or False?

3 Lewis Clarke works for Friends of the Galapagos, a nature conservation charity. Read his email to the manager responsible for tourism in the region and answer the questions.

1 How is tourism different from in the past?

2 What is his opinion of ecotourists?

3 In what way does he feel the islands are at risk?

From:	Lewis Clarke
To:	Beatriz Garcia

Dear Beatriz,

As you know, the islands are no longer on Unesco's list of World Heritage sites in danger. Personally, I find this absurd as there now more than 40 species under threat from ecotourists.

1 Unlike visitors 30 years ago, who were accommodated by local residents, these so-called ecotourists now require more comfort and book their stay through foreign tour operators. As a result, local enterprises cannot compete and only 15 percent of tourism income remains in the local economy. The cruise ships operating in the Galapagos are basically floating hotels and few passengers stay in guesthouses or eat out.

2 An increase in flight arrivals and the growth of sports such as sea kayaking, scuba diving and fishing are also a threat to the islands' biodiversity. People sailing from island to island make it more difficult to prevent the introduction of new invasive alien species that take over from the indigenous flora and fauna.

We urgently need to meet to discuss the danger tourism represents not only to the island's fragile ecosystem but also to its financial sustainability.

Lewis

Listening

DEALING WITH THE THREATS

4))) **4.3** Listen to a meeting held at the offices of the Galapagos National Park Administration to discuss the points raised in Lewis' email. Correct the mistakes in the secretary's notes.

Environmental concerns meeting

- visitor numbers: sometimes controlled; 11,600 total; past 40 years mainly on islands Isabela, Santa Cruz and San Cristobal
- invasive species: too late to do anything; invasion of cats: will bring report next meeting
- pleasure boats: number of luxury pleasure boats should be cut; half of tourist income leaks away

GRAMMAR: REPORTING VERBS

We use **reporting verbs** to relate what someone has said.

1 Many reporting verbs are followed by *that*: *acknowledge, confirm, deny, feel, observe, point out, state, suggest.*

*She **acknowledged/denied/stated that** there was a problem.*

2 Other reporting verbs are followed by *to* + infinitive: *agree/disagree, claim, promise, threaten.*

*He **promised to bring** a full report to the next meeting.*

3 Others are followed by an object + *to* + infinitive: *advise, persuade, remind, tell, urge, warn.*

*She **advised/reminded/urged them to take** immediate action.*

See Grammar reference, pages 112 and 113.

5 Study the Grammar box and complete the minutes of the meeting from Exercise 4 with reporting verbs. The first letter of each verb is given to help you.

Minutes

Present: Lewis Clarke, Friends of the Galapagos; Beatriz Garcia, Galapagos National Park Administration; Fernando Cordero, Santa Cruz Pleasure Boats; James Baldwin, Charles Darwin Research Facility

BG opened the meeting by ¹r_____ everyone that visitor numbers are strictly monitored. She ²s_____ that the number of ship passengers, the duration of their stay and sites visited are recorded meticulously. She also ³p_____ o_____ that each ship receives a compulsory site schedule from the park and visitors are not allowed free access to sensitive sites.

LC ⁴a_____ that this scheme had been beneficial but ⁵f_____ that there should be an annual limit to the number of tourists. He ⁶w_____ that the present situation was unsustainable and ⁷u_____ the meeting to take action to protect the islands from further degradation. JB ⁸c_____ that this was indeed the case and was worried about the recent invasion of rats brought in on board passenger ships. He ⁹p_____ to give an update on pest control at the next meeting.

FC ¹⁰d_____ with the others that there was any immediate need to deal with the pest problem but ¹¹s_____ that the number of luxury yachts owned by foreign tour operators should be drastically reduced and ¹²o_____ that the local economy failed to benefit from the influx of tourists.

PROFESSIONAL SKILLS
CHAIRING A MEETING

Reading

THE KEY TO SUCCESSFUL MEETINGS

1 What needs to be done to ensure that a meeting is successful? Think about the elements in the box and their role in the success or failure of a meeting.

> the agenda   the discussion   the role of the chairperson

2 Read the text and find FOUR reasons why meetings can be frustrating. Then make a list of the elements of a successful meeting mentioned in the text.

Top tips for successful meetings

Why do meetings fail? Sometimes meetings may go on too long, leading to boredom and lethargy. Sometimes they are badly organized – no agenda has been circulated, the discussion goes round in circles and no one ever finds common ground or reaches agreement. Nobody takes minutes, so the next meeting is all about deciding what was decided during the last meeting. On other occasions, the chair dominates the discussion and the other participants are not allowed to get a word in.

The key to a successful meeting lies in the chairperson's skill in running it smoothly. He or she is responsible for calling the meeting, stating its purpose and ensuring that the discussion is relevant to the points raised on the agenda and that everyone can contribute. Enough time should be allotted to each topic and if one issue begins to dominate or people begin to digress, the chair must take back control. Sometimes it will be necessary to come to a decision, put the matter to the vote and then move on to the next topic. The chairperson may occasionally have to remind participants to remain polite, not interrupt or monopolize the discussion. Finally, it is up to the chair to bring proceedings to a close, summarize the main points, state what action is now required and then set a date for the next meeting.

Vocabulary

VERB + NOUN COLLOCATIONS

3 Match the verbs 1–10 with the phrases a–j to make expressions from the text.

1 set	**a** something to the vote
2 circulate	**b** a meeting
3 come	**c** round in circles
4 reach	**d** a point
5 go	**e** agreement
6 find	**f** to a decision
7 take	**g** an agenda
8 raise	**h** common ground
9 put	**i** a date
10 call	**j** minutes

4 Why do you think chairing a meeting might be difficult? Discuss with a partner. Then complete the advice in the Professional skills box with the correct form of the verbs in the box.

> allow   appoint   dominate   ensure   keep   put   set   state

PROFESSIONAL SKILLS: CHAIRING A MEETING

Dos

1 ¹_____ the purpose of the meeting.

2 ²_____ a secretary to ³_____ the minutes.

3 ⁴_____ the discussion does not digress.

4 ⁵_____ the issues to the vote.

5 ⁶_____ a date for the next meeting.

Don'ts

6 ⁷_____ the meeting to go on indefinitely.

7 ⁸_____ or monopolize the discussion.

Listening

THE SINKING OF THE *MS DISCOVERY*

5 You will hear part of a meeting about the sinking of the *MS Discovery* after it hit an iceberg in the Antarctic. What do you think happened when the ship sank? Discuss with a partner, using the words in the box. Use a dictionary if necessary.

> chemicals   crew   garbage   hull   lifeboat
> mainland   rescue   rocks   sonar   vessel

6 Work in pairs. Look at the participants on the right and the organizations they represent. Predict who or what they might be most concerned about in relation to such accidents.

7)))4.4   Listen to the meeting. Are the statements true (T) or false (F)?

1 The aim of the meeting is to agree who was responsible for the accident. T / F

2 The rescue ship arrived three and a half hours after the incident. T / F

3 The *MS Discovery* has started to leak oil into the sea. T / F

4 The *MS Discovery* was equipped with sonar to detect obstacles underwater. T / F

5 The lifeboats did not provide adequate protection against the weather. T / F

6 One cruise ship was previously fined $18 million for polluting the seawater. T / F

8 How well did the chairman conduct the meeting? Tick (✓) the things he did. You can look at audio script 4.4 on page 120 to help you.

1 ___ call the meeting to order

2 ___ state the purpose of the meeting

3 ___ allow all participants to contribute

4 ___ prevent irrelevant debate

5 ___ summarize the discussion

6 ___ call for a vote

Writing

MINUTES OF A MEETING

9 Look at audio script 4.4 on page 120 and write the minutes of the meeting. Use the model in the Writing bank on page 97 to help you.

Professor Fernando Morales, Chairman, Antarctic Protection Agency

Barbara White, Antarctic Protection Agency

Dr Howard, Australian Marine Research Centre

Richard Baxter, Friends of the Sea

Tanya Olsen, Friends of the Sea

CASE STUDY
DEVELOP AN ECO-RESORT

CASE STUDY MENU

Aim: To hold a meeting to discuss an ecotourism project.

1 Read about the Brijuni Archipelago.

2 Listen to an interview about an eco-resort development.

3 Hold a meeting to discuss the issues involved in the project.

4 Come to an agreement and write a summary of the meeting.

The Brijuni Archipelago

1 **Read the extract from a travel blog and answer the questions.**

1 What could attract people to Veliki Brijun?

2 To what extent is the wildlife at risk from the influx of tourists?

3 How satisfied are tourists with their stay?

THE BRIJUNI ARCHIPELAGO

Mali Brijun

Veliki Brijun

DK

The Brijuni Archipelago

The Brijuni Archipelago consists of 14 islands situated three kilometres from the mainland of Istria in Croatia. Visitors are only permitted to stay on the biggest island, Veliki Brijun.

The climate is mild and the combination of sunny weather and high humidity has produced a lush and luxurious vegetation. There are 700 plant species, 250 different birds and many varieties of fish and shellfish on the islands. There are some endangered species but their breeding colonies are protected by conservation laws. Adult turtles can often be seen basking in the sun and if visitors are lucky, they may spot Brijuni's famous pink dolphins.

The Brijuni National Park was created in 1983 and boasts a zoo and safari park. There are three luxury hotels on Veliki Brijun with spacious suites and sea views. There are opportunities for yachting, water skiing and deep-sea diving, and the annual Watersports Festival is a popular attraction. However, although many visitors enjoy their stay, some travel blogs claim that the hotel facilities are too modern, the rooms are monotonous and the outdoor activities are more or less the same as anywhere else.

climate = ภูมิอากาศ   monotonous = ซ้ำจำเจ

endangered = สัตว์ใกล้สูญพันธุ์   Lush = เขียวชอุ่ม

A self-catering eco-resort

2))) **4.5** Listen to a representative of the Croatian Tourist Board, the mayor of Mali Brijun and a representative of the Croatian Wildlife Association talking about the creation of a self-catering eco-resort and tick (✓) the topics that are discussed.

a ✔ job creation   e ___ building works

b ✔ overseas investment   f ✔ benefits to the community

c ___ tax revenues   g ✔ visitor numbers

d ✔ invasive foreign species   h ✔ preservation of the environment

3))) Listen again and number the topics in Exercise 2 in the order you hear them. What points do the speakers make about these topics?

TASK

4 The representative of the Croatian Tourist Board has called a meeting to discuss the project and circulated an agenda. Work in groups of three. Read the agenda below and your role cards and prepare to meet the other participants. Student A, look at the information below. Student B, turn to file 5, page 103. Student C, turn to file 12, page 105.

5 Roleplay the meeting. Discuss the issues and try to come to an agreement about the project.

Agenda

1 presentation of the project
2 advantages of the development
3 the way forward

Student A

You are a representative of the Croatian Tourist Board. You will chair the meeting and present the extract below from a report prepared by the board. Try to enlist support for the project.

Report: eco-resort on Mali Brijun

The New Project Committee has decided to launch an eco-resort on the island of Mali Brijun. The resort will be built in two phases:

1 The construction of a jetty and road for access to the resort. This involves clearing approximately 20 hectares of forest. The wood will be used to build accommodation on the island.

2 The construction of 35 chalet bungalows with modern facilities and an outdoor swimming pool.

15% of energy needs can be generated by wind turbines and solar panels. Each bungalow will be built by local contractors and covered with vegetation.

All year round activities will include boating and fishing. A marina will be built for yachts and pleasure boats (providing rental income). Nature trails and cycling paths through the forest will be created, including four bird observatories.

Over 200 dinosaur footprints have been discovered on the island and a private group of investors is interested in financing a dinosaur theme park.

Meeting summary

6 One of your colleagues was unable to attend the meeting. Write an email (200–250 words) to him/her, summarizing the discussion of the project.

UNIT 4: KEY WORDS

biodiversity   conservation   disembark
disposal   ecosystem   endangered species
garbage   indigenous   influx   leakage
recycling plant   siphon off   sourcing
stakeholder

See DVD-ROM Mini dictionary

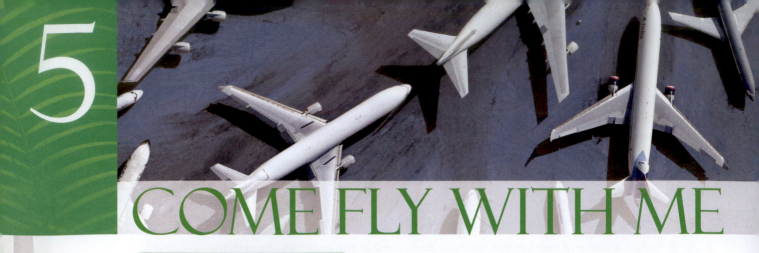

5

COME FLY WITH ME

Reading

WHAT MAKES A GOOD AIRPORT

1 **What makes a good airport? Discuss with a partner. Consider the facilities and services airports provide.**

2 **Read the article about modern airports on page 41 and complete it with sentences a–g.**

  a And, for a reasonable fee, the Dutch airport even hosts weddings.

  b The thought crosses my mind every time I pass through London Heathrow's disorganized Terminal 3.

  c For me, Changi is the **benchmark** for what an international airport should be: an airport you and your family actually want to spend time in and enjoy yourself.

  d But if, unlike me, you would rather spend minimal time in the terminal, could our opinion of airports change if they found more creative ways to keep us amused with new, customer-focused amenities?

  e And if there was more focus around the customer and differentiation, we'd be more likely to return and spend money: a win-win for all?

  f Wouldn't we be more inclined to pay a small price for a **dedicated** airport agent to arrange our onward coach, bus or airline transportation at our destination than pay for a trolley, for example?

  g Of course, some of you may spare little thought for what's on offer at airports.

3 **Complete the sentences with the words in bold in the article in Exercise 2.**

  1 There's a(n) _____ agent who is responsible for identifying passengers who need to check in rapidly.

  2 Last-minute deals often enable you to purchase _____ tickets.

  3 Vienna's Schwechat International Airport has an east-west _____ with a capacity of 24 million passengers.

  4 Some people prefer a(n) _____ mobile phone to a yearly subscription plan.

  5 Your insurance covers baggage that is lost or damaged _____.

  6 Our airline meals are the _____ by which all in-flight catering should be judged.

4 **Work in pairs. Choose some words from the article in Exercise 2 that you have not seen before and look them up in a dictionary. Read the definitions to your partner for him/her to identify the words.**

What makes a good airport?

On my last holiday I tumbled down an indoor helter-skelter, relaxed in a tropical butterfly garden, swam in a rooftop pool and my children had fun in a forest-themed indoor playground. And all of this was just at the airport.[1]___ Could the bustling hub of Singapore Changi be the ultimate 21st century airport for the consumer **in transit**, the 'transumer'?

[2]___ Heathrow is more of a chaotic factory churning out passengers than an airport to be cherished, with none of the 'fun' diversions that many Asian airports offer to woo the weary traveller waiting for a flight. For example, Hong Kong's Chek Lap Kok Airport is a great place to play a round of golf between flights, while Kuala Lumpur International offers passengers fresh air in a giant rainforest inside the terminal.

[3]___ Most people tend to judge an airport more on its security, service and ability to handle delays and cancellations efficiently than on whether it has spa treatments or independent cafés. [4]___ Such creative people-oriented facilities that might encourage travellers to arrive at the airport earlier could include texting coupons to our mobiles for a **discounted** meal or spa treatment. Or a guided tour providing an insight behind the scenes of how an airport functions. At the very least, offering free wi-fi as standard. [5]___

Amsterdam Schiphol is another good example of an airport offering something for everyone. The Netherlands' **hub** has just opened the first 6D theatre at an airport and is also well-stocked with unique attractions from flower shops to a library, museum, indoor/outdoor garden and casino. [6]___

Although airports cannot always offer their attractions for free, what's stopping them from offering us 'optional' **pay-as-you-go** services that complement the airline and benefit us? [7]___ Even if we have to pay a little extra, these services are what airports should be looking at as a foundation for improving our experience. If we have to spend two hours navigating our way around a 'fortress', we should have the opportunity to get the best out of our time there. Until then, I'll save my holiday money for my next trip via Changi, where I'm hoping for a roller coaster that will propel me to my gate. And who knows? It might actually happen.

Listening

THE PASSENGER EXPERIENCE

5))) 5.1 **Listen to four passengers talking about the kind of airport they appreciate. Match the speakers 1–4 with the subjects they talk about a–d.**

Who talks about:

a queues? ___ **b** airport design? ___ **c** transport links? ___ **d** signage? ___

6))) **Listen again. What suggestions do the speakers make regarding each of the items in Exercise 5?**

RESEARCH

Do an internet search for good and bad airports. Choose one and present it to the class.

AIRPORT SECURITY

Reading

SECURITY REGULATIONS

1 Work in pairs. Are the following statements about airline regulations true (T) or false (F)?

1 Handbags count as one item of carry-on luggage. T / F

2 Any bag containing a gel or cream is subject to separate inspection. T / F

3 Lighters can only be placed in baggage destined for the hold. T / F

4 Passengers have to justify their possession of any medication. T / F

5 Security staff have to taste any baby food before allowing it through security. T / F

6 Security staff may use their own discretion in enforcing the regulations. T / F

2 Read the passenger security regulations and check your answers in Exercise 1.

Passenger security regulations

- Each passenger is restricted to one item of cabin baggage with a maximum size of 56 cm x 45 cm x 25 cm. Other bags, such as handbags, may be carried within the single item of cabin baggage.
- All liquids should be put in hold baggage. This includes water and other drinks, creams, sprays, pastes and gels. Liquids, gels and aerosols are only allowed in individual containers of 100 ml, which must fit comfortably in one, transparent, resealable bag no larger than 20 cm x 20 cm. The bag must be presented separately for examination at airport security.
- One lighter per person may be taken through the search point but must not be placed into the cabin bag after screening – it must be carried on the person for the entire flight. Lighters are not authorized in hold baggage.
- Essential medicines may be permitted in larger quantities above the 100 ml limit but are subject to authentication. Passengers are obliged to bring supporting documentation from a qualified medical professional.
- Liquid baby food or sterilized water can be taken through airport security. The accompanying adult will be required to verify by tasting.
- Laptops and other large electrical items have to be removed from cabin baggage and screened separately.
- Security personnel are not permitted to deviate from these regulations. While you are being searched, do not joke about having a bomb or firearm in your possession. Penalties can be severe and include the possibility of being sent to prison and/or fined.

GRAMMAR: THE PASSIVE

1 **The passive** is often used in official, impersonal statements, when the focus is on the action to be performed.

2 To form the passive, use the appropriate tense of the verb *be* + a past participle.

Present simple	*Lighters **are not authorized** in hold baggage.*
Present continuous	*A new air traffic control system **is being installed**.*
Past simple	*He **was denied** entry because his passport had expired.*
Present perfect	*Since 9/11 stricter border controls **have been enforced**.*
Past perfect	*He complained because his medicine **had been confiscated**.*
Will	*A new body scanner **will be installed** next month.*
Future infinitive	*A new terminal **is to be built** next year.*

3 It is possible to use modals with passive verb forms:
*Everything possible **will/should/must** be done to ensure a swift passage through immigration.*

See Grammar reference, page 113.

3 Study the Grammar box. <u>Underline</u> all the examples of the passive in the security regulations in Exercise 2. Circle the examples of modals used with the passive.

4 Which examples indicate:

a an obligation?

b a recommendation?

c a possibility?

5 Read the description of the baggage handling process and change the verbs in italics into the passive if necessary.

Baggage handling: frequently asked questions

When you check in, your itinerary ¹*displays* on the computer and one or more bag tags ²*print out*. These ³*attach* to each of your pieces of luggage.

The tag has all of your flight information on it, including your destination and any stopovers, as well as a bar code containing a ten-digit number. This number is unique to your luggage and ⁴*can use* by the computers in the baggage-handling system to look up your itinerary.

After check-in the numbers ⁵*read* by an automated scanner. This device ⁶*can scan* the bar codes on about 90 percent of the bags that ⁷*pass by*. The other bags ⁸*route* to another conveyor to ⁹*scan* manually. Once the 10-digit bar code number ¹⁰*has identified*, each bag ¹¹*takes* to its appropriate destination.

If a conveyor ¹²*obstructs* in any way, your baggage will ¹³*route* around the blockage.

Finally, your baggage ¹⁴*loads* onto a destination-coded vehicle and ¹⁵*sorts* at a sorting station next to the gate. The bags ¹⁶*transfer* onto carts and ¹⁷*take* the short distance to the waiting plane to ¹⁸*place* in the cargo hold.

PROFESSIONAL SKILLS
DEALING WITH DIFFICULT SITUATIONS

Listening

PROBLEMS AT CHECK-IN

1 In your experience, what are the most common problems passengers face at check-in? Discuss with a partner.

2)) 5.2 Rachel Hoffmann is the ground staff supervisor for AVA Airlines at Heathrow airport. She is discussing some recent difficult incidents with the check-in desk staff. Listen and complete the incident report form.

Incident report form

Person involved	Situation	Action taken
Karen		
Steve		
Tadzio		

3 Compare your answers in Exercise 2 with a partner and discuss the questions.

  1 How well do you think the members of staff handled the different situations?

  2 What different ways of handling each situation would you suggest?

4 Complete the summaries of the incidents from Exercise 2 in your own words. Then look at audio script 5.2 on page 121 and check your answers.

  1 A large group of pax was about to check in. The parents were unable [1]_____ children and started [2]_____ about [3]_____. Their baggage [4]_____ floor and the other pax [5]_____. Dalal was asked [6]_____ and finish the check-in procedure.

  2 At first I refused to allow a passenger onto the flight as check-in [7]_____ previously. However, his wife [8]_____ and the captain [9]_____.

  3 Justyna was on duty and a passenger became abusive and [10]_____. Tadzio, who was on the next counter, defended her and [11]_____ face. As a result, he [12]_____ for two weeks. Although [13]_____ from the passenger, he [14]_____ and will not [15]_____.

5 Complete the advice in the Professional skills box with the correct form of the verbs in the box.

> assume   avoid   listen   provide   reassure   respond   take

PROFESSIONAL SKILLS: DEALING WITH DIFFICULT SITUATIONS

Dos

1 _____ the passenger has a right to be upset.

2 _____ carefully and show empathy and consideration.

3 _____ an explanation and an apology.

4 _____ the passenger that you will do your best to find the best possible outcome.

Don'ts

5 _____ a complaint as a personal attack.

6 _____ to emotion with emotion.

7 _____ taking responsibility by making excuses for your company's shortcomings.

NO MORE FLIGHTS TONIGHT

6))) 5.3   **Listen to a customer service agent for a flight delivering some bad news to passengers and answer the questions.**

1 Which dos from the Professional skills box does he observe?

2 Identify THREE expressions he uses to try to calm the passengers down.

3 Do you think he succeeds in calming the passengers down? Why/Why not?

4 Identify any mistakes he makes.

Speaking

CALMING PASSENGERS DOWN

7 **Work in small groups. Look at the exchanges between the customer service agent (A) and the passengers (P). Write improved versions and act them out.**

P1: We've been waiting here all day. What I want to know is whether you'll be refunding the transfers at the other end.

A: I can't tell you that.

P1: And the hotel?

A: I can't say that.

P2: Why can't you?

A: I'm sorry. I fully understand how you feel.

P3: Are you going to get me to Frankfurt this evening?

A: I can't.

P3 Why not?

A: I'm very sorry for the inconvenience but there are no more seats.

P3: Why not?

A: There are no more seats.

P3: Why not? I want an answer!

A: I have no control over the situation. I'm just passing on information.

8))) 5.4   **Now listen to improved versions of the exchanges and compare them with the ones you wrote. How are they better than the exchanges in Exercise 7?**

9 Work in pairs. Student A, turn to file 6, page 103. Student B, turn to file 22, page 108. Use the information to roleplay the two situations. Then discuss how successful you were in calming the passengers down and providing a satisfactory solution.

RESEARCH

Conduct a survey using interviews and the internet to find out more about the most common problems airport staff have to deal with. Report back to the class.

CASE STUDY
DEVELOP AIRPORT INFRASTRUCTURE

CASE STUDY MENU

Aim: To decide on a strategy for developing an airport's infrastructure.

1   Read an article about a small regional airport.
2   Listen to a meeting about a number of issues.
3   Hold a meeting to discuss the potential developments.
4   Make recommendations and write up the minutes.

Claybourne Airport

1   Read the article from a magazine for airline industry professionals and answer the questions.

1   Which airlines use Claybourne Airport?
2   Why has the airport grown so fast?
3   What problems has this growth caused?

Claybourne Airport – a victim of its own success?

Claybourne Airport is a small regional airport handling about 3.2 million passengers a year. It was originally a military airfield which was purchased by a consortium of local government authorities in 2004, when a major programme of building work and runway investment was begun. The airfield was renamed 'Claybourne', to reflect the nearby cities of Claythorpe and Glenbourne which it serves, and it opened for passengers in April 2006.

The arrival of low-cost carriers in 2010 resulted in a sharp jump in passenger numbers, rising 36 percent in that year. RedBird Airlines established a hub in 2011 and the operation has been strengthened since the airline's absorption by BeeLines, which flies to a range of domestic and European short-haul destinations.

However, the increase in passenger flows has been causing congestion both landside and airside, and the Regional Airport Authority in conjunction with BeeLines is now looking into other issues that have arisen for the airport. According to RAA Chief Executive Nigel Foreman, 'We're a victim of our own success. We now need to work out how to increase capacity, improve the airport's facilities and passenger handling, while at the same time turning in a healthy profit.'

Development issues

2   ))) 5.5   Listen to a conversation between representatives of the Regional Airport Authority and BeeLines to discuss a number of issues. Number the topics in the order you hear them.

a ___ facilities
b ___ air traffic control
c ___ personnel
d ___ capacity
e ___ passenger handling
f ___ transport

3   )))   Listen again. What is the main issue or challenge with regard to each of the topics in Exercise 2?

TASK

4 Work in small groups. You are going to hold a meeting to try and find a solution to the problems at Claybourne. Read the agenda on the right and try to think of as many ideas as possible for each of the items. Group A, look at the information below. Group B, turn to file 9, page 104.

5 Roleplay the meeting. Appoint a secretary and discuss the items on the agenda. Decide on a five-point action plan to solve Claybourne's problems.

Agenda

1 check-in procedures
2 airport expansion
3 human resources
4 safety and security
5 revenue stream

Group A

CONFIDENTIAL: Ministry of Interior

A report submitted to the Ministry of Interior suggests that criminals are exploiting airlines' self check-in systems to travel using false identities. At present domestic passengers are able to check in and drop off luggage without having to present any proof of identity.

The report recommends abandoning e-ticketing and conducting ID verifications at check-in so that only passengers can pass through security lines – as is the case at international terminals.

From:	Arthur Scarman, TWGU
To:	Claybourne Airport Management

There are rumours that you are planning to reduce labour costs by introducing even more job 'flexibility', i.e. making people do tasks that are not part of their job description and for no extra pay.

Given the failure of recent talks on improved salary and working conditions, we will be calling on airport and security staff who belong to our union to strike for an indefinite period as from next Wednesday.

Revenue at Claybourne Airport

- Fees paid by BeeLines for the runways, aircraft stands, landing charges and cargo are down 1.6 percent over the last five years in real terms.
- Fees for facilities (e.g. retail, parking, rental space): projected increase of 18 percent, accounting for 65 percent of total income.

Plane Absurd pressure group blocks airport taxiway

The campaign against the new runway at Claybourne entered a new phase yesterday, when community activists, local residents and climate change campaigners prevented aircraft from taking off for over five hours. In a communiqué, the group stated that aviation's contribution to climate change is expected to rise to 17 percent by 2050 with disastrous global-wide consequences.

A spokesman for the campaign said, 'The traffic around here is horrendous and the motorway is congested. It's impossible to sleep with all the aircraft flying overhead. There should be a curfew on all night flights. And a new runway would make it worse, especially if it's long enough for Boeing 747s and Airbus A380s. We won the case at Beaconsfield and we'll win this one too.'

Minutes of the meeting

6 Write the minutes of the meeting you have just held. Use the model in the Writing bank on page 97 to help you.

UNIT 5: KEY WORDS

aircraft stands   benchmark   bump up   carrier
cart   conveyor   ground handling crew   hold (n)
hub   landing charges   landside   pay-as-you-go
pax   screening   slots   turnaround times

See DVD-ROM Mini dictionary

REVIEW AND CONSOLIDATION

Tourism developments

1 **Read the text about family travel. <u>Underline</u> all the verb forms which indicate a changing or developing situation.**

'Have Kids Still Travel'

Family travel is becoming more and more popular. The majority of those who travel with children is in the Generation X category, aged 26 to 39, but now that the population in many countries is getting older, many grandparents are travelling with their grandchildren as well.

Children are increasingly playing an influential role in choosing where to go on holiday, and their interests and desires seem to be an important factor in parental choice. Travel brings the family closer together and although travel dates still revolve around the children's school holidays, more and more surveys are revealing that parents are prepared to take their children out of school for short periods of time to avoid higher fares and congestion.

Continuous aspect

2 **Circle the correct options in italics. Sometimes more than one option is possible.**

1 At the moment many new hotels *are built* / *are being built*.

2 Medical tourism is a sector that *grows* / *has been growing* rapidly in recent years.

3 Many jobs *are created* / *are being created* in the hotel industry at the present time.

4 The castle *converts* / *is being converted* into a residential conference centre.

5 Tourists *now become* / *are now becoming* more critical and the demand for better quality service *has increased* / *has been increasing*.

6 Next month we *will offer* / *will be offering* a special discount on weekend breaks to Venice.

7 The cost of living *has risen* / *has been rising* rapidly over the last six months.

8 People who *travel* / *are travelling* frequently *may fulfil* / *may be fulfilling* a desire to escape their cultural background.

Ups and downs

3 Circle the option in italics that is wrong or does not make sense in each sentence.

1 Festival goers boosted passenger numbers *gradually / significantly* during the week of the arts festival.

2 Looking at the graph, I am struck by the *slight / dramatic* surge in reservations in July.

3 Passenger traffic dipped *steadily / slightly* last weekend compared to the same weekend last year.

4 Airlines have had to contend with a *modest / sharp* hike in fuel prices, up by 15 percent.

5 The number of overseas visitors went up in the last quarter and is still *on the rise / levelled off*.

6 Job growth in the travel industry has *outpaced / declined* all other sectors of the economy.

Advertising and publicity

4 Are the following advertising (A) or publicity (P)?

1 a television commercial broadcast during prime time   A / P

2 a message about an upcoming event posted on Twitter   A / P

3 space purchased for a banner embedded in a commercial website   A / P

4 a television documentary about cruise holidays   A / P

5 the sponsorship of a local charity by a travel organization   A / P

Countable and uncountable nouns

5 Are the words in bold countable (C) or uncountable (U)?

1 She's an expert in software **design**. C / U

2 You should always make a back-up **copy** of your files. C / U

3 How much money do you spend on **promotion**? C / U

4 Despite the media **hype**, I found the new smartphone very disappointing. C / U

5 We've purchased some **space** for an **advertisement** in the magazine. C / U, C / U

6 When she was a student, she kept a record of her **travels** on the Indian subcontinent. C / U

7 We did a **promotion** at the trade fair and gave away lots of travel vouchers. C / U

8 **Advertising** is the art of convincing people to spend **money** they don't have for something they don't need. C / U, C / U

Web words

6 Find 13 words connected to websites in the word square. Then use them to complete the sentences.

T	L	E	O	P	I	B	L	O	G	N	H
C	R	A	S	H	Y	O	A	F	M	Y	G
V	C	R	C	W	R	E	F	R	E	S	H
Q	U	X	R	L	K	S	E	K	E	O	E
S	K	L	O	A	D	S	F	O	N	T	Z
E	M	L	L	P	P	T	Y	R	F	M	S
A	E	U	L	A	Y	O	U	T	E	N	H
R	N	A	E	F	L	B	P	C	N	E	E
C	U	R	S	O	R	A	L	I	N	K	A
H	A	K	U	U	Q	F	O	J	W	T	D
J	D	L	U	U	P	M	A	F	E	P	E
F	B	A	N	D	W	I	D	T	H	Q	R

1 He posts regularly on his travel _____. It's a great place to pick up tips about Asian travel.

2 Why does this computer always _____ and I lose everything I've been working on?

3 Why don't you _____ the screen and see if there's any new content?

4 This website is taking an awfully long time to _____. There must be some huge images!

5 The most readable _____ is often said to be *Helvetica*.

6 The _____ of text and graphics on the page should be given careful consideration.

7 Use your mouse to place the _____ at the start of the first row, then type in your name.

8 Click on the _____ below to find out more about our terms and conditions.

9 It will take a while to _____ that video onto your site – it's huge!

10 These video files are too big to put up on the site – we don't have enough _____.

11 Bing and Google are the most popular _____ engines.

12 You need to _____ down the page to find the information you're looking for.

13 We need an eye-catching _____ at the top of the page to draw the user in.

Making predictions

7 Complete the text about San Francisco with the words in the box.

> bound to   chances are   could   likelihood   probably won't   unlikely to

There is [1]_____ be a major earthquake in San Francisco sooner or later and [2]_____ that it will occur in the next few decades. In 1980 a federal report declared the [3]_____ of a major earthquake hitting California within the next 30 years was 'well in excess of 50 percent' and yet the Big One has yet to strike. While on holiday in California, most tourists are [4]_____ give the idea of an earthquake happening a second thought. Yet California has more than 300 faults running beneath its surface, so while you're there, it's possible that you [5]_____ feel the earth move, even if you are so busy doing other things that you [6]_____! Nevertheless, the Big One is coming – there's no doubt about it.

The business plan

8 Complete the advice about creating a business plan with the words in the box.

> bottom line   brand identity   break even   cater for   forecasts   niche
> overview   profit and loss   public relations   threats

Your business plan is like a road map giving you clear directions to where your business is heading. Here are a few stages to help you on your journey.

1 The name of the game
  What your business is called is part of its [1]_____, so make it memorable and easy to recognize and repeat.

2 The mission statement
  What will your business be like in five years' time? Will you expand it to include other branches or extra employees? Write a paragraph for the website with a concise [2]_____ of what is unique about your business idea and makes it stand out from the competition.

3 The marketing plan
  Clearly define your territory and [3]_____. What kind of public will you [4]_____? How will you promote your product or service? What are your proposals for advertising and [5]_____?

4 SWOT analysis
  Outline your strengths, as well as opportunities and [6]_____. Point out what weaknesses there may be in your financial [7]_____ but don't undersell yourself or you may put off potential investors.

5 The [8]_____
  A business can operate without budgets but your bank manager will certainly want to see your [9]_____ statements for the first year. Your accountant will draw up an initial balance sheet to give you some idea of how long it will take to [10]_____ before you can start making a profit.

Branded vs boutique

9 Complete the paragraph with the words in the box.

> attentive   distinctive   intimate   stylish   uninspiring

The branded hotel we stayed at in New York was totally bland and [1]_____ but we ate out in a very [2]_____ Art Deco restaurant on Madison Avenue with a very cosy and [3]_____ atmosphere. Next time we'll book into a 'lifestyle' hotel with a(n) [4]_____ personality and [5]_____ personnel who will look after all our needs.

Word formation

10 Complete the text with a word formed from the word in capitals at the end of the line.

Throughout the resort, there are many multinational hotels and ¹_____ of profits is therefore high, with foreign products being ²_____ in to satisfy guests' ³_____. The host community benefits minimally from tourism because the lion's share of the hotel chains' profits is ⁴_____ to external stakeholders. There is growing ⁵_____ within the Goan population over this state of affairs. Protests have been held over the ⁶_____ behaviour of visitors, the ⁷_____ damage caused by waste and the excessive use of scarce resources. This kind of mass tourism in the region is clearly ⁸_____.	LEAK FLY REQUIRE TRANSFER CONTENT APPROPRIATE ENVIRONMENT SUSTAIN

Key word transformations

11 Complete the second sentence so that it has a similar meaning to the first sentence using the word given. Use between two and five words, including the word given.

1 'There should be a drastic reduction in access to sensitive sites,' Beatriz said.
suggested

Beatriz _____ access to sensitive sites.

2 Luis told the meeting that action had to be taken immediately. **urged**

Luis _____ immediately.

3 She said that she thought the number of visitors should be strictly monitored.
recommended

She _____ numbers.

4 The cruise operator told the captain not to sail too close to the coast. **warned**

The captain _____ too close to the coast.

5 Could you stick to the point because this discussion is getting nowhere? **circles**

Could you stick to the point because we are _____?

6 We need to decide now if you don't want to stay here all night. **reach**

We need to _____ you want to stay here all night.

Dealing with difficult passengers

12 Complete the words in these sentences. The first letter of each word is given.

1 We will do our u_____ to find a satisfactory solution.

2 I'm very sorry for any i_____ that has been caused.

3 There's no need to get angry – please c_____ d_____.

4 The circumstances are b_____ our control.

5 I'm explaining the situation to you; I'm not making e_____.

6 I h_____ what you're saying and I fully understand your point of view.

7 I'm sorry but I'm just the messenger – I'm just p_____ on the information I've been given.

8 I'm going to give you a form to fill in so you can c_____ on the insurance.

The passive

13 Rewrite the sentences using the passive form of the verbs in brackets.

1 You cannot put lighters in hold baggage. (authorize)

e.g. *Lighters are not authorized in hold baggage.*

2 They didn't allow him to enter because his passport had expired. (deny)

3 They have imposed stricter border controls. (enforce)

4 She complained because they had taken away her medications. (confiscate)

5 They are introducing a new air traffic control system. (install)

6 There is a limit of one item of cabin baggage per passenger. (restrict)

6

HERITAGE

UNIT MENU

Grammar: talking about the past
Vocabulary: describing a heritage site, architecture, guiding expressions
Professional skills: working as a tour guide
Case study: Ascoby Hall – design a museum exhibition

Reading

WORLD HERITAGE SITES

1 **Match the photos A–F with the texts 1–6 about famous World Heritage sites. Then circle the correct options to complete the texts.**

1 Lake Baikal lies in ___, near the city of Irkutsk. It is the world's deepest and oldest lake and contains 20 percent of the planet's unfrozen freshwater. The lake supports an outstanding variety of flora and fauna of exceptional value in the study of evolution.
a Southern Siberia   **b** Northern Kazakhstan   **c** Belarus   **d** Lapland

2 The Altamira Caves, situated 30 kilometres west of ___, contain some of the world's finest examples of prehistoric art. The earliest engravings and drawings date back to around 16,000BCE. They feature on the World Heritage List as masterpieces of creative genius and as humanity's earliest accomplished art.
a Torrelavega   **b** Santander   **c** Salamanca   **d** Zaragoza

3 The Sydney Opera House is considered to be one of the greatest architectural works of the 20th century. Located downtown and overlooking the harbour, it was conceived and built by ___, who won the competition for the best design back in 1957. The construction comprises three groups of interlocking vaulted shells, covered by over one million white tiles in a chevron pattern.
a a Danish architect, Jørn Utzon   **b** an American architect, Frank Gehry
c a British architect, Norman Foster   **d** a Chinese-American architect, I.M. Pei

4 The 93 Senegambia stone circles consist of over ___ monuments carved out of laterite and erected between the third century BCE and the 16th century AD, forming a vast landscape of ancient graves and burial mounds. The survival of so many circles is a unique manifestation of a sophisticated and prosperous society.
a 500   **b** 1,000   **c** 1,500   **d** 15,000

5 When Mount Vesuvius in the Gulf of Naples erupted in 79CE, it buried the ancient towns of ___, as well as many luxurious villas in the area. The ruins were excavated as from the 18th century and give a fascinating and unparalleled insight into life in the early Roman empire.
a Rome and Pompeii   **b** Pompeii and Napoli   **c** Pompeii and Herculaneum
d Pompeii and Stabiae

6 The spectacular ice-carved fjords, lakes and valleys in Te Wahipounamu, ___, are amongst the finest landscapes in the Southern Hemisphere. 'Te Wahipounamu' is a Maori term meaning 'the place of greenstone'. Greenstone was used for tools, weapons and ornaments, and was believed to have spiritual force.
a Fiji   **b** Rarotonga   **c** Tahiti   **d** New Zealand

2 Work in pairs. Read the texts in Exercise 1 again. Take turns to ask and answer the questions below for each one.

1 What criteria justify their inscription as World Heritage sites?   **3** What can be seen at the site?

2 Are any significant dates mentioned?   **4** In which country is the site located?

Vocabulary

DESCRIBING A HERITAGE SITE

3 <u>Underline</u> these expressions for talking about heritage sites in the texts in Exercise 1. Then find another example for each category in the texts.

Where	When
... lies in ...	... as from the 18th century ...
Located downtown ...	... date back to around 16,000BCE.
Features	**Significance**
... carved out of laterite ...	... give a fascinating and unparalleled insight into ...
The construction comprises ...	... some of the world's finest examples of prehistoric art.

4))) 6.1   Study the Grammar box. Then listen to some more information about Pompeii and Altamira and complete the examples.

> ### GRAMMAR: TALKING ABOUT THE PAST
>
> **1** Use **used to** and **would** to refer to repeated past events.
> *The sons of many of the noble and rich families* ¹_____ *Pompeii as well as Rome and Venice.*
> *Given the enthusiasm for all things Italian, visitors* ²_____ *artists to paint original works, landscapes and city views.*
> *All of the paintings are of animals such as deer that the cave dwellers* ³_____ *all around them.*
>
> **2** Use **it is believed/said/thought that** to refer to events which are not necessarily historically accurate but are generally accepted to be true.
> *We don't know why they painted them but* ⁴_____ *that they may well have had some magic significance.*
> *I personally doubt this but* ⁵_____ *that they had been painted by shamans.*
> See Grammar reference, pages 113 and 114.

5 Rewrite the sentences using the words in brackets.

1 People say that the stone circles at Stonehenge were used for the purposes of astronomy. (said)
e.g. *It is said that the stone circles at Stonehenge were used for the purposes of astronomy.*

2 It was a custom for the ancient Egyptians to bury their dead with a list of magic spells and instructions for the afterlife. (used)

3 There is some evidence that the Megalithic Temples of Malta are the oldest buildings in the world. (thought)

4 People suppose that Napoleon may have died from arsenic poisoning. (believed)

5 In the Middle Ages sieges went on for months and could even last for years. (would)

6 Groups of Homo Sapiens and Neanderthals lived in close proximity but in separate communities. (used)

Writing

WORLD HERITAGE AT HOME

6 Choose a World Heritage site in your country and write a short description of the site (250–300 words). Use the model in the Writing bank on page 98 to help you.

ST PETERSBURG

Speaking

ST PETERSBURG

1 **What do you know about the Russian city of St Petersburg, which is a UNESCO Heritage site? Circle the correct options in italics to complete the sentences. Compare your ideas with a partner.**

1 The city was founded by *Peter the Great / Peter II of Russia / Catherine the Great*.

2 It was built on a *disused coal mine / swamp / public park*.

3 Which of these buildings is not associated with St Petersburg?
the Hermitage / Menshikov Palace / the Spasskaya Tower

4 The city has changed its name *twice / three times / four times*.

5 The city was besieged and many buildings were destroyed in *1848 / 1917 / 1941–1944*.

Reading

THE WINTER PALACE

2 **Read the extracts from a tour guide to the Winter Palace, one of the most famous buildings in St Petersburg, and answer the questions.**

Which part of the building (A–E):

1 has an impressive roof? _____

2 contains a piece of English furniture? _____

3 was used for hospital beds? _____

4 was the scene of an annual ceremony? _____, _____

5 is associated with the Russian revolution? _____

6 is most typical of Rastrelli's style? _____

One of the most famous buildings in St Petersburg is the Winter Palace. It was built in the fashionable baroque style for Tsarina Elizabeth (1741–1762), the daughter of Peter the Great, and was designed by the Italian architect Francesco Bartolomeo Rastrelli.

C

The Small Throne Room was dedicated in 1833 to the memory of Peter the Great and houses a silver English throne made in 1731. Diplomats gathered here on New Year's Day to offer good wishes to the Emperor.

A

The Armorial Hall, with its immense pillars, bronze chandeliers and slender colonnade supporting the balcony and its balustrade, covers over 800 m². An infirmary was set up here during the First World War.

D

The Rotunda is a circular hall in the northwest wing of the palace, created for Tsar Nicholas I. It served as an antechamber and connected the public rooms with the intimate quarters used by the imperial family in the west wing. It is topped by an impressive dome.

B

The Malachite Room, richly decorated with malachite columns and ornate vases, gilded doors and ceilings, and a parquet floor, was used during the revolution of 1917 as the seat of the provisional government before the Bolsheviks took power.

E

The Main Staircase, a vast, white marble staircase was the architect's best work. In the 18th century the staircase was known as the Ambassadorial Staircase because the representatives of foreign countries used it when going to the palace. On 6th January each year the Tsar would descend the staircase in full imperial attire for the ceremony of the Blessing of the Waters of the River Neva.

Listening

THE GOLD DRAWING ROOM

3))) **6.2** **Listen to Sonia, a tour guide, during her tour of the Winter Palace and circle the adjective in each list that she uses to describe the noun in bold. Which adjective in each list cannot be used with the noun in bold?**

1 **ceiling:** painted / wood-beamed / delicate / plaster / vaulted

2 **chandeliers:** gilded / gold-plated / bronze / silver / brick

3 **columns:** vast / immense / parquet / massive / marble

4 **vases:** ornate / velvet / elegant / finely-wrought / ornamental

4))) **Listen again and answer the questions.**

1 What does Sonia say about Alexander II?

2 What does she say about Maria Alexandrovna?

Vocabulary

ARCHITECTURE

5 **Look at the pictures of the architectural features below and <u>underline</u> the odd word in each group. Explain your choice. Use a dictionary to help you.**

1 arch / column / colonnade / pillar

2 cupola / dome / façade / tower

3 arcades / apartments / chambers / quarters

4 balcony / balustrade / gallery / mantelpiece

5 bas-relief / minaret / spire / steeple

6 vestibule / antechamber / entrance / wing

7 gilded / silver / bronze / parquet

balustrade

minaret

arch

pillar

dome

spire

cupola

colonnade

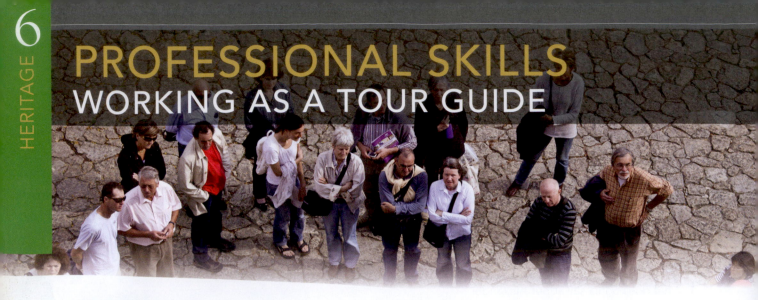

PROFESSIONAL SKILLS
WORKING AS A TOUR GUIDE

Listening

GUIDING

1))) **6.3** Amy Wood works for an agency that trains English-speaking tour guides in Russia. Listen to her introduction to the course and complete the Professional skills box. Use no more than THREE WORDS in each gap.

PROFESSIONAL SKILLS: WORKING AS A TOUR GUIDE

Personal qualities

To be a good guide, you have to be:

1 friendly, helpful and able to cope with ¹_____.

2 enthusiastic, with a good sense of ²_____ and a(n) ³_____ personality.

3 in good physical condition and have plenty of ⁴_____.

4 aware of and ⁵_____ the needs of all members of the group.

Knowledge

You also need to:

5 prepare everything in advance and have all the details ⁶_____.

6 avoid being monotonous and try to be ⁷_____ possible.

7 ⁸_____ about any interesting events that took place there.

8 take advantage of every opportunity to ⁹_____ interesting information.

Communication skills

When you take people around a site:

9 speak in a(n) ¹⁰_____ and ¹¹_____ voice so that people can hear you.

10 use non-verbal communication, make ¹²_____ and use appropriate ¹³_____.

Vocabulary

GUIDING EXPRESSIONS

2 **Match the sentence halves 1–8 with a–h.**

1 The visit will take an hour and you'll see	**a** our steps to the main staircase?
2 If you could all be back here	**b** our way to the kitchens and servants' quarters.
3 I suggest we	**c** of 18th century baroque architecture.
4 If you'd like to	**d** by 5.30 at the latest.
5 Now we'll make	**e** follow me into the east wing.
6 On your left you'll see a beautiful example	**f** make our way to the courtyard.
7 Why don't we retrace	**g** back to the Armorial Hall?
8 Shall we head	**h** the museum's most precious items in the Treasure Galleries.

3 **Match the sentence halves 1–8 with a–h .**

1 Saint Petersburg was founded
2 The statue was erected to commemorate
3 The Hermitage was inaugurated
4 The interiors were subsequently altered
5 Catherine the Great was inspired
6 An infirmary was set up in the Hall
7 The antique furniture was restored
8 Sadly, the palace was burnt down

a by Baroque architecture.
b during the First World War.
c by a cabinet maker in Moscow.
d by Peter the Great.
e by a number of different architects.
f by a huge fire in 1837.
g as a public museum in 1852.
h the battle of Kagul in 1770.

Listening

DATES, MEASUREMENTS, STATISTICS

4))) 6.4 **Tour guides often have to talk about dates, measurements, statistics, etc. Practise saying the figures below with a partner. Then listen and check your answers.**

1 1,346 ft tall
2 1941–1943
3 15 m x 35 m
4 250,000 years ago

5 2.57 m high
6 2001
7 ¾ of an inch thick
8 6/1/1546

9 75,000,000 visitors
10 $16.90
11 2nd century BCE
12 4,954,000

Speaking

A WALKING TOUR

5 **You are going to give a walking tour of the district shown on the map. Prepare your tour using the prompts below. Imagine the outside and inside of the buildings and monuments, their history and cultural heritage.**

1 originally built for ..., acquired by ..., designed in ... style, today forms part of ...
2 outside/inside ..., initially home to ..., boasts a fabulous collection of ...
3 scene of a dramatic event ..., depicts ..., revolution, annual parade
4 erected by ... to commemorate ..., decorated, restored
5 commissioned by ..., inspired by ..., made of ..., represents ...
6 destroyed by ..., centre of ..., World Heritage site because ...
7 founded ..., inaugurated ..., completed ..., 150 rooms containing ...
8 the former ..., is said to be ..., terrible event ..., today houses ...

6 **Give your tour to the class. Use the guiding expressions in Exercise 2.**

CASE STUDY
DESIGN A MUSEUM EXHIBITION

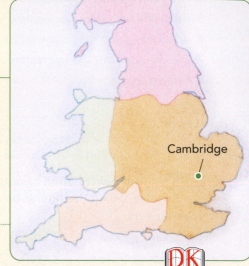

CASE STUDY MENU

Aim: To design a museum exhibition.

1 Read an article about a gift to a museum.
2 Listen to a meeting about a collection of artefacts.
3 Sort artefacts into categories.
4 Plan the layout of exhibits and write supporting documentation.

A present from the past

1 Read the newspaper article. What does the collection include and what decisions have to be made?

Local Donington man donates museum collection

Albert Johnson, 79, a resident of Donington with a lifelong interest in local history, has donated his collection of artefacts and objects of historical interest to the Donington Trust, which intends to house them in nearby Ascoby Hall. The building has been empty for a number of years.

The priceless collection spans 2,000 years of life in East England, with items ranging from whalebone combs to windmills. Particularly well-represented are the many objects dating back to the time when the area was settled by the Vikings. A number of possessions belonging to the locally-born explorer Matthew Flinders (1774–1814) will also be among the exhibits on display.

The newly-appointed curator of Ascoby Hall told our reporter that plans are underway to design the layout of the exhibition in the limited space available. 'We can't house everything, so we have some difficult decisions to make. We need to assess the relative importance of each of the artefacts and decide how to display them, based on their intrinsic significance and ability to appeal to the public.'

A meeting to discuss the display

2))) 6.5 Listen to the curator of Ascoby Hall and an interior designer talking to Albert Johnson about organizing the exhibition space and answer the questions.

1 What were the rooms available for the exhibition originally used for?
2 What ideas do the curator and the interior designer have for the use of the rooms?

3))) Listen again and answer the questions about the people in the pictures.

Who:

1 built Ascoby Hall? ___
2 lived at Ascoby Hall? ___
3 installed a stained glass window? ___
4 founded the Gentlemen's Society? ___
5 was a genius? ___
6 was a sailor? ___
7 went to Australia? ___
8 wrote an important book? ___

Sir Isaac Newton

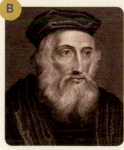
Geoffrey Johnson

Tobias Johnson

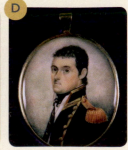
Matthew Flinders

Sorting the exhibits

4 **Put the words in the box in FIVE groups and give a name to each group. Use a dictionary if necessary.**

| axe   bracelet   brooch   ~~clay~~   compass   helmet   model   pendant   ~~pot~~ |
| replica   reproduction   sextant   shield   telescope   ~~vase~~ |

Pottery	_____	_____	_____	_____
e.g. *clay*				
pot				
vase				

5 **Work in pairs. Student A, look at the information below. Student B, turn to file 23, page 108. Look at your inventories and decide how best to group all the objects into EIGHT different categories for the eight rooms in the museum. There is one object you do not need. Follow the steps below.**

1 Identify the objects in your inventory. Put them into groups according to periods of history (e.g. Roman, Saxon, 18th century) or types of activity/areas of interest (e.g. drainage, local language).

2 Compare your results with your partner. Discuss and see what common groups you can make.

3 Finalize your eight groups and decide on a name for each one.

Student A

Inventory

- a life-size replica of a Viking longship
- an 18th-century telescope, compass and sextant
- a large map of the Australian coastline (1801–1803)
- five combs carved from whalebone (circa eighth century)
- a 1.5 x 1 m photo of excavations of a Roman salt-making site
- photos of the great floods in 1947 and 1953
- a first edition of Isaac Newton's *Principia Mathematica*
- ten silver pendants and brooches originating from Sweden
- manuscripts dating back to Saxon times
- medieval kitchen utensils and bronze keys
- models of windmills and steam engines used to pump water
- a collection of surgical instruments used on board ships

TASK

6 **Work in small groups. You are going to design the layout of the museum. Discuss the questions and make decisions.**

1 What names will you give the rooms?

2 What kind of articles will you sell in the gift shop?

3 How can you make the museum attractive to visitors, including children?

7 **Draw a museum plan and then use it to present your exhibition to the class. Explain your group's plans for the success of the museum.**

UNIT 6: KEY WORDS

artefact   bas-relief   commemorate   dome   excavate   inaugurate   masterpiece   monument   prehistoric   replica   ruins   shield   stained glass   throne   wing

See DVD-ROM Mini-dictionary

7

MANAGING EVENTS

Listening

THE ROLE OF AN EVENTS COORDINATOR

1)) **7.1** Listen to Emma Murray talking about her work and complete the job profile below.

> **Name:** Emma Murray   **Age:** 27
> **Job title:** ¹_____   **Place of work:** ²_____
> **Professional qualifications:** ³_____   **Working hours:** ⁴_____
> **Main responsibilities:** ⁵_____, ⁶_____

2)) Listen again and answer the questions.

   1 What THREE examples does Emma give of problems she has had recently?

   2 How did she deal with each problem?

Vocabulary

COLLOCATIONS WITH *EVENT*

3 The verbs in the box can all be used with *an event*. Find the four pairs of synonyms.

> call off   cancel   celebrate   mark   postpone   put off   put on   stage

4 Complete the sentences from the recording in Exercise 1 with the correct form of a verb from Exercise 3. Then look at audio script 7.1 on page 123 to check your answers.

   1 I don't just ¹_____ events for the club – although that's part of it.

   2 What I do is ²_____ events for other people using the club's facilities.

   3 If anyone wants to ³_____ a special occasion like a product launch or hold a private party, they can use the club as a venue.

   4 The match was ⁴_____ 15 minutes before the game was due to start because the pitch was frozen.

   5 Luckily, I had some alternative entertainment prepared just in case they decided to ⁵_____ or ⁶_____ the game.

GRAMMAR: HYPOTHETICAL SITUATIONS

1 Use the **third conditional** (*if* + past perfect and *would/could/might have* + past participle) to talk about hypothetical situations in the past.

*If I **had known** in advance, I **would have arranged** for an interpreter.*

*If I **hadn't anticipated** the bad weather, I **wouldn't have had** a contingency plan.*

*They **could have played** the match **if** the pitch **had been covered** beforehand.*

*We **might have found** a better venue **if** we **had done** some more research.*

2 We can often talk about a hypothetical situation in the past with a result in the present.

*If he **hadn't missed** his train, he**'d be** here by now.*

3 In formal styles, *if* can be dropped and the auxiliary verb placed before the subject.

Had I realized how important it was, I would have reacted more quickly.

See Grammar reference, page 114.

5 Match the sentence halves 1–6 with a–f. Then complete the sentences with the correct form of the verbs in brackets.

1 I _____ (order) more tables and chairs

2 If I _____ (not had) a contingency plan,

3 If the weather _____ (be) better,

4 We _____ (cancel) the event

5 If I _____ (not check) the equipment beforehand,

6 If she _____ (check) with me previously,

a if too few people _____ (registered).

b the keynote speaker's microphone _____ (not work).

c if you _____ (tell) me you needed them.

d she _____ (know) what to do now.

e we _____ (set up) a marquee outside.

f there _____ (be) a disaster.

Speaking

WHAT WENT WRONG?

6 Work in small groups. Read the email. Then think about the problems and discuss what you could, would or might have done about them.

> Emma,
>
> I've had some feedback about last weekend's conference. Apparently, there were some hiccups: one of the four conference speakers failed to show up and one of them was so boring that the delegates were taking phone calls during his presentation. I'm told that there was traffic congestion on the roads to the venue, so half the delegates had not yet turned up by ten o'clock, when the first speaker was ready to begin.
>
> Some of the exhibitors have complained that they weren't given enough space and were forced to set up displays blocking the emergency exits. There was also an incident when one of the delegates fell down the stairs and was unconscious for several minutes. Nobody knew what to do and the one person trained in first aid had gone missing. It seems too that some of the temporary staff you recruited didn't know where they were supposed to be.
>
> Could you please think of how these problems could have been avoided and how you would deal with similar issues in the future?

RESEARCH

Choose a sports venue in your area (e.g. a football club). Find out what corporate hospitality packages are available, what they offer the client and how much they cost. Present your findings to the class.

EVENT CONCEPT

Listening

THE FIVE Ws

<table>
<tr><td>Location:
Essaouira is situated on the Atlantic Coast of Morocco, 113 km (70 miles) from Agadir and 170 km (106 miles) west of Marrakech.</td></tr>
<tr><td>When:
The festival takes place each year over four days at the end of June.</td></tr>
<tr><td>Visitors per year:
450,000</td></tr>
</table>

1))) **7.2** The five Ws are questions that an events manager asks at the beginning of a new project. Listen to Part One of an interview with Hamza Habri, an organizer of the Gnawa festival in Essaouira, Morocco, and complete the questions.

1 Why _____?

2 Who _____?

3 When _____?

4 Where _____?

5 What _____?

2))) Listen again. What answers does Hamza give to the questions in Exercise 1?

3 Complete the sentences from the interview in Exercise 1 with the words in the box. Then look at audio script 7.2 on pages 123 and 124 to check your answers.

> backs   coordinate   forward planning   host community   liaises
> logistics   mission statement   showcase   sponsor   stand to gain

1 For every major event like this one, if it is going to be a success, you need a vision and a ^{1}_____.

2 So, for us, the mission is to ^{2}_____ Gnawa music and dance.

3 There are many different stakeholders. First of all, the ^{3}_____ because there were over 450,000 visitors last year.

4 The Ministry of Tourism is involved in programming the event and ^{4}_____ with the town of Essaouira.

5 The people manning the stalls in the fish market, the hoteliers, the people providing bed and breakfast accommodation – all these ^{5}_____.

6 And I mustn't forget our main ^{6}_____, the BMCE bank, which ^{7}_____ the festival financially.

7 There are so many things to ^{8}_____ and it involves a great deal of ^{9}_____.

8 One of the hardest things about ^{10}_____ is looking at a list and spotting what is not there.

4))) **7.3** Event managers often use *SMART* objectives as a planning tool. Listen to Part Two of the interview and write what *SMART* stands for.

1 S = _____

2 M = _____

3 A = _____

4 R = _____

5 T = _____

5))) What examples does Hamza give for each type of *SMART* objective? Discuss with a partner. Then listen again and check your answers.

RESEARCH

Use the internet to find out about the WOMAD (World of Music, Arts and Dance) festival and events held in different parts of the world every year. Think about:

• what WOMAD's mission is.

• where and when the festival is held.

• what activities are organized during the festival.

Reading

AN EVENT BRIEF

6 Chris Hamilton is the CEO of an American corporation called Smartset, which makes mobile phones. Read the event brief he has sent to Apotheosis, an events management company and tick (✓) the correct answers.

SMART**SET**

   1 What are the objectives of the event?
     a ___ to celebrate the firm's results
     b ___ to thank personnel for their hard work
     c ___ to roll out a new product
     d ___ to raise awareness of the brand

   2 Which requirements does he mention?

a ___ catering	**d** ___ location	**g** ___ security
b ___ control of costs	**e** ___ media coverage	**h** ___ transport
c ___ live music	**f** ___ pre-planning	**i** ___ parking

> ## Event brief
>
> **To: Events Coordinator**
>
> **1** The aim of the event is to throw a party for Smartset employees and their guests. The objective is to celebrate the success of the different branches and also to reward staff for their role in the company's achievements over the past year.
>
> **2** The venue should be accessible from the major employee sites of Oakland (where the majority work), Alameda and Rockridge. Last year we held an outdoor concert attended by most of our 950 employees. 85 percent of those who were there expressed satisfaction in the feedback questionnaire and this year we aim to exceed expectations.
>
> **3** The programme of entertainment should appeal to our staff, whose average age is under 30. Refreshments should be provided, taking into account different dietary considerations.
>
> **4** The events management company selected will take on temporary serving staff, organize security arrangements, liaise with the press and/or television, etc. at their own expense.
>
> I suggest we set up a joint task force to discuss the event in greater detail and come up with some good ideas. When we have a better idea of the overall cost and reach agreement on terms and conditions, we will be in a position to draw up a contract and set things in motion.
>
> Chris Hamilton
>
> PS I will, of course, be making an introductory speech.

Speaking

DESIGNING AN EVENT

7 Work in pairs. Student A, turn to file 10, page 104. Student B, turn to file 24, page 109. Roleplay a meeting to draw up an initial plan for the organization of the Smartset corporate event. Remember to use the *SMART* objectives.

PROFESSIONAL SKILLS
UNDERSTANDING CONTRACTS

Reading

LEGAL MATTERS

1 Work in pairs. Make a list of the main legal issues that you would have to think about as an events manager. Compare your ideas with another pair.

PROFESSIONAL SKILLS: UNDERSTANDING CONTRACTS

The language used in contracts has a number of features:

1 adverbial expressions with *here*, e.g. *hereinafter* (= later in this document).

2 formulaic language, e.g. *whereas* (= considering that), *it is agreed as follows*.

3 the use of *shall*. In legal documents, *shall* means 'must'.

4 two equivalent words joined by *and*, e.g. *terms and conditions, covenants and agreements*.

5 the use of *such*. In legal documents, *such* refers back to a previously mentioned noun.

6 long sentences. This is often owing to a desire to be all-inclusive so that no eventuality is omitted.

---

2 Study the Professional skills box. Look at the Event Planner Agreement on page 65 and underline examples of legal language. Find TWO more examples of 1, 2 and 4.

3 Read the Event Planner Agreement again and answer the questions.

Which article in the Event Planner Agreement deals with:

1 unforeseen occurrences? ___

2 responsibility for planning the event? ___

3 purchasing goods or services from external suppliers? ___

4 information not to be communicated to third parties? ___

5 advertising the event? ___

6 permission to use copyright material? ___

7 the governing law in case of dispute? ___

8 transferring contractual obligations to other companies? ___

4 Complete the sentences with the legal expressions in the box.

---

accept and agree   consent and approval   costs and expenses
null and void   terms and conditions

---

1 The purchaser shall be liable for all [1]_____, including insurance and delivery.

2 Both parties hereby [2]_____ to all the [3]_____ contained hereinabove.

3 Any substantial breach will hereby render the contract [4]_____.

4 Neither party shall assign any of the said rights and obligations without the prior [5]_____ of the other party.

Event Planner Agreement

ARTICLE 1: OBJECT OF THE AGREEMENT

1.1 The Event Planner shall provide the services described hereunder in Appendix A attached.

...

1.3 The Event Planner shall be responsible for the organization and management of all details necessary for the performance of services outlined in Appendix A, including but not limited to the Event site, negotiating any and all leases or obtaining any permits and licences, parking, insurance, rental or leasing of any equipment and negotiating any fees and services to be outsourced to any contractor, vendor or service provider.

...

ARTICLE 2: CONFIDENTIALITY

...

2.2 Each party shall keep in strict confidence all commercial and technical information in whatever form acquired and use its best endeavours to bind its employees and agents to do the same.

...

2.5 The Event Planner hereby accepts and agrees to use the Company's name, logo or trademark in any material used by the Event Planner in promotion of the Event, including but not limited to any announcements in newspapers, magazines, billboards, on the internet or in radio and television announcements and for no other purpose without the prior written consent of the Company.

...

ARTICLE 4: ASSIGNMENT

4.1 Neither party shall have the right to transfer any of its rights or obligations under this Agreement to any other company, firm or person without first obtaining the consent and approval in writing of the other party, which consent shall not be unreasonably withheld. Any breach of this term shall render the contract forthwith null and void.

...

ARTICLE 5: FORCE MAJEURE

5.1 Neither party shall be considered in default in the performance of its obligations under the terms and conditions of this Agreement, or be responsible for any failure or delay in the execution of such obligations if the performance thereof is prevented or delayed wholly or in part as a consequence, whether direct or indirect, of any cause beyond the reasonable control and without the fault or negligence of such party.

...

ARTICLE 6: JURISDICTION

6.1 The provisions of this Agreement shall be construed and the performance thereof governed in accordance with the laws of the State of New York, USA.

...

IN WITNESS THEREOF, the parties, intending to be legally bound, have executed this Agreement as of the date first above written.

Signed for and on behalf of

_____   _____

Speaking

FINALIZING ARRANGEMENTS

5 Work in groups of three. Student A, look at the information below. Student B, turn to file 7, page 103. Student C, turn to file 14, page 105. Roleplay a meeting between Smartset's CEO and two events coordinators with Apotheosis.

Student A

You are Smartset's CEO. Work with Students B and C to decide on the final content and cost of the Smartset event.

- You have an initial budget of $40,000.
- You want your employees to have a good time but are anxious to keep down the cost.

Writing

CONTRACT DETAILS

6 Complete Appendix A referred to in Article 1.1 of the contract above with details of the agreement you reached in Exercise 5. The appendix should include a detailed description of all services to be performed by the event planner. Use the model in the Writing bank on page 99 to help you.

CASE STUDY
MAKE A FESTIVAL PROFITABLE

MALAYSIA

CASE STUDY MENU

Aim: To help a music festival to become profitable

1 Read about the Asia Sound music festival.

2 Listen to an interview with the festival organizer.

3 Read some messages about problems.

4 Brainstorm ideas on how to make the festival a success.

Asia Sound

1 Read the article published in the music magazine *Jookbox* about the Asia Sound festival and answer the questions.

1 Why did Nick Ikin create the festival?

2 What difficulties has the festival run into?

Sounds of silence for Asian music festival?

The Asia Sound music festival was founded in 2008 by Nick Ikin, the bass guitarist of the defunct Australian band The Burning Pagodas. Their music was a mix of punk, dub and Asian rhythms but they never made it big. Says Nick, 'I used to sometimes run into people who liked bands from southeast Asia but we were few and far between, so I thought it would be great to go out there and create a festival that would make some of these groups known on the international stage.'

The festival is now a success, with an annual parade led by the legendary Malaysian Drummers Dance Band but last year was marred by scenes of violence, when gatecrashers pushed through the barriers and attacked security guards. Local residents also protested at the noise generated by the event held in a park near a residential area and the failure of the organizers to clean up the site. A number of cases of food poisoning were also reported.

There are serious questions hanging over the organizers of next year's festival. Two years ago 35 people were seriously injured in a front-of-stage crush. Many bands have complained that their fee is too low and are reluctant to perform. Lack of money is a major issue – the festival made a loss of AUD 321,000 last year and the main Australian sponsor, Yarwood Pty, has threatened to pull out unless things improve.

An interview in *Jookbox*

2))) 7.4 Listen to a journalist from *Jookbox* magazine interviewing Nick Ikin and tick (✓) the correct answers.

1 Which of the difficulties mentioned in the article does Nick talk about?

a ___ excessive noise
b ___ finance
c ___ food poisoning
d ___ gatecrashers
e ___ violence

2 What are the solutions he proposes?

a ___ sales of CDs
b ___ a different venue
c ___ extra staff
d ___ a benefit concert
e ___ more police

3 How confident is he about this year's festival?

a ___ unsure
b ___ optimistic
c ___ over-confident

Some bad news

3 **Read the messages Nick has received and answer the questions.**

1 Which messages refer to:
   a a misunderstanding?   **c** non-payment?
   b an improved offer?   **d** a withdrawal of support?

2 What effect will these changes have on the upcoming festival?

3 What should Nick do to ensure the festival can still take place?

1 Sorry, mate. Cambodia Dub Foundation are not doing Asia Sound this year. We've got a better deal at Kuala Lumpur Live with a 25 percent better fee. Hope you get a replacement.

2 **Final reminder**

Unless the outstanding sum of AUD 30,000 owed to my clients, The Java Jive All Stars, for their performance at last year's Asia Sound festival is paid by the 30th of this month, we will be obliged to seek recovery through the courts.

Yours sincerely,
Rebecca Logan, Ellis & Hunt, International Law Firm

3 It is with regret that I have to inform you that Yarwood is no longer in a position to sponsor the Asia Sound festival. We no longer wish to be associated with an event which we feel does not enhance our reputation. We wish you every success for the forthcoming festival.

4 Just had Nami Tamaki on phone. Wants 15% more or she won't play. Speak 2 u l8r. Bill

5 Hi,

After the interview I got a whole lot of emails and texts from listeners who say they don't want Asia Sound to be held in a stadium. They say it would turn the festival into a sit-down concert and that's not the experience they want. Any ideas?
Simon, *Jookbox* magazine

6 Dear Mr Ikin,

I am writing further to our recent phone conversation as I feel we were talking at cross purposes. I did not intend to allow you to use our stadium without payment. The fee for the second weekend in July would be AUD 75,000. Please contact me if you are still interested.

Razak Bin Osman, Kuala Lumpur Football Club

TASK

4 Work in pairs. Student A, turn to file 8, page 103. Student B, turn to file 26, page 109. Roleplay a meeting between Nick and a representative of Global Productions, an events management company. Draw up a plan for how the festival can take place in the best conditions without losing money.

UNIT 7: KEY WORDS

attendance   breach of contract
contingency plan   coordinate   draw up
null and void   put on   put off   roll out
set in motion   stage an event   signage
sponsorship   task force   upcoming

See DVD-ROM Mini dictionary

8

CAREERS

Speaking

STARTING YOUR CAREER

1 How many different ways of finding a job can you think of? Which do you think are the most/least successful? Discuss the questions with a partner.

Listening

FINDING A JOB

2))) **8.1** Listen to four people talking about how they found work in the travel industry. Match the speakers 1–4 with the methods they used a–j. Which methods are not mentioned?

a attending a job fair ___

b being headhunted ___

c using online web portals ___

d through friends and family ___

e targeting a specific company ___

f using a temporary employment agency ___

g targeting a number of different companies ___

h belonging to a professional association ___

i using professional networking sites ___

j responding to newspaper advertisements ___

3))) Listen again and match the extracts from the recording 1–8 with the job search methods a–j in Exercise 2.

1 … it's very time-consuming. ___

2 … most of them never replied … ___

3 … and offered to do a three-month internship without pay. ___

4 I joined the Institute for Personnel and Development. ___

5 … it wasn't specifically targeted towards tourism … ___

6 I even included a video of myself. ___

7 … the jobs advertised weren't specific enough. ___

8 But I was very lucky because one day and quite by chance … ___

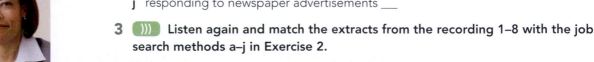

Reading

APPLYING FOR A JOB

4 Work in groups of three. Student A, look at the information below. Student B, turn to file 13, page 105. Student C, turn to file 25, page 109. Read your job advertisements and exchange information to complete the table below. Which job appeals to you most?

Skirun.com is a leading web retailer specialized in the sale of ski and snowboarding holiday packages. As a result of recent growth in our business, we are recruiting a **ski sales manager**.

Reporting to the international sales director, you will be responsible for leading a team of reservation consultants specialized in ski holidays to European and North American ski resorts. Duties include training new recruits, briefing staff on new products and organizing daily work schedules.

The ideal candidates will be computer-literate, possess excellent organization skills, have a keen eye for detail and previous telesales experience. You will also be outgoing, energetic, autonomous, able to work in a pressurized environment and have a good knowledge of ski holiday destinations.

We offer a competitive salary, uncapped commission, free winter holidays and excellent career prospects.

Please email your CV and covering letter detailing your experience to recruit@ski-run1.com

Company name	Skirun.com	On-TrackTours	Howatt Hotels
company activity			
job title	e.g. *ski sales manager*		
role and responsibilities			
candidate profile			
remuneration			

5 Rewrite the sentences replacing the <u>underlined</u> parts with language from the three job advertisements in Exercise 4.

1 The candidate must be <u>able to use a computer</u>.

e.g. *The candidate must be computer-literate.*

2 He/She must have a <u>well-developed ability to notice precise information</u>.

3 The ideal candidate must be able to <u>do many things at once in a stressful situation</u>.

4 The person appointed must have <u>substantial experience</u> in the industry.

5 He/She must be <u>able to work on his/her own</u> and <u>concerned to maintain quality</u>.

6 The candidate should <u>speak well</u> and <u>have sold from a call centre before</u>.

7 Responsibilities include <u>carrying out</u> interviews and <u>helping decide who to appoint</u>.

8 The ideal candidate will have <u>an excellent ability to direct and supervise other people's work</u>.

Vocabulary

REMUNERATION

6 Write your own definitions for the terms below, then check with a dictionary.

1 commission
2 fringe benefit
3 discount
4 profit-sharing
5 stock option scheme
6 salary
7 performance-related pay
8 fees
9 wages
10 retirement savings scheme

Speaking

JOB SATISFACTION

7 Work in pairs. What factors, apart from salary, motivate you in a job? Make a list of factors and put them in order of importance. Discuss the reasons for your choices. Then tell your partner about your ideal job.

SELLING YOURSELF

Speaking

YOUR PERSONAL PROFILE

1 Tick (✓) the five words that describe you best. Cross (✗) the five words that describe you the least. Use a dictionary if necessary. How do you think these qualities will be useful in your future career in tourism?

___ adventurous	___ critical	___ methodical	___ responsible
___ ambitious	___ determined	___ outgoing	___ sensitive
___ cautious	___ hard-working	___ passionate	___ stubborn
___ competitive	___ helpful	___ perfectionist	___ tactful
___ conscientious	___ imaginative	___ reliable	___ talented
___ considerate	___ impatient	___ reserved	___ thorough
___ creative	___ loyal	___ resourceful	___ versatile

2 Work in pairs. Tell your partner about yourself and give examples to justify your description.

Listening

WRITING A CV

3))) 8.2   Listen to a human resources manager, a careers advisor and a former student talking about writing CVs. Match the speakers 1–3 with the things they talk about a–f.

Who talks about:

a describing skills? ___   **d** acronyms and abbreviations? ___

b the length of a CV? ___   **e** recreational activities? ___

c a photograph? ___   **f** customizing the CV? ___

4)))   Listen again and identify SIX things job applicants should do and SIX they shouldn't do.

Should do	Shouldn't do
e.g. *print on good-quality paper*	

Speaking

THE PERFECT CV

5 Work in small groups. Discuss the elements of a perfect CV and present your conclusions to the class.

6 Look at the CV in the Writing bank, page 100. To what extent does it meet the requirements of a good CV?

7 Study the Grammar box. Write at least FIVE sentences describing yourself using some of the dependent prepositions.

e.g. *During my internship I was responsible for dealing with enquiries.*

I take pride in being conscientious and methodical.

GRAMMAR: DEPENDENT PREPOSITIONS

1 **Prepositions** can be dependent on verbs, adjectives or nouns. Use the *-ing* form of a verb after a preposition or prepositional phrase.

*Personally, I don't **object to seeing** a photo.*

*I am **good at working** under pressure.*

*I see **little point in attaching** my CV if you aren't going to read it.*

2 It is possible to use a possessive pronoun before the *-ing* form:

*If you don't meet the selection criteria, there's little likelihood **of your getting** the job.*

3 Here are some dependent prepositions:

- **Verbs:** *apply for, benefit from, concentrate on, look forward to, object to, specialize in, succeed in, work at*
- **Adjectives:** *aware of, conscious of, eligible for, familiar with, good at, interested in, keen on, responsible for*
- **Nouns:** *attempt at, benefit to, experience in, likelihood of, opportunity for, pride in, question of, track record in*

See Grammar reference, pages 114 and 115.

Writing

COVERING LETTERS

8 **Read the covering letter for the job of ski sales manager from Exercise 4, page 69 and circle the correct options.**

Dear Mr Kennedy,

I am writing to apply ¹___ the position of ski sales manager which was ²___ on the Jobs in Tourism website (http://jobsintourism.au/job/954703).

   I am ³___ working for a winter sports tour operator and have a proven track record ⁴___ dealing with the public. I am applying because I am interested ⁵___ pursuing a career in sales and ⁶___ my advanced computer skills to benefit the company.

   As you will see from the ⁷___ CV, I have considerable ⁸___ in reservations and working under pressure. I am also used to ⁹___ with the managers of other departments in order to further company goals. I have a proven ¹⁰___ record in the skiing holiday industry and have always succeeded ¹¹___ a team. In addition, I speak English, Spanish and German fluently.

   I will be available for interview from next week. Meanwhile, please do not hesitate to contact me if you require further information.

   I look forward to ¹²___ from you.

Yours sincerely,

Giovanni Maldinia

1 **a** to	**b** on	**c** at	**d** for
2 **a** advertised	**b** appeared	**c** presented	**d** show
3 **a** typically	**b** currently	**c** eventually	**d** hopefully
4 **a** to	**b** by	**c** in	**d** with
5 **a** at	**b** by	**c** in	**d** with
6 **a** to use	**b** using	**c** to match	**d** matching
7 **a** connected	**b** enclosed	**c** included	**d** mentioned
8 **a** experience	**b** experiences	**c** opportunity	**d** practicality
9 **a** liaise	**b** liaising	**c** succeed	**d** succeeding
10 **a** background	**b** experience	**c** track	**d** involvement
11 **a** to motivate	**b** with motivating	**c** by motivating	**d** in motivating
12 **a** read	**b** reading	**c** hear	**d** hearing

RESEARCH

Do an internet search to find advertisements for the kind of job(s) you are interested in.

How do they describe the following?

a the company

b the responsibilities

c the profile of the ideal candidate

d the pay and prospects

PROFESSIONAL SKILLS
INTERVIEWS

Listening

PREPARING FOR AN INTERVIEW

1 Work in pairs. Make a list of dos and don'ts for before, during and after a job interview.

2))) 8.3 Listen to Stephen Lang, a human resources manager, talking about going for an interview and answer the questions.

   1 What points does he mention for before and during the interview?

   2 What does he suggest doing after the interview?

Speaking

HANDLING INTERVIEW QUESTIONS

3 Match the sentence halves 1–8 with a–h in the Professional skills box to make eight difficult interview questions.

> ### PROFESSIONAL SKILLS: INTERVIEWS
>
> | | |
> |---|---|
> | **1** How would a friend or colleague | **a** why we should hire you? |
> | **2** Could you briefly run through | **b** to be your greatest strength? |
> | **3** What do you consider | **c** describe you? |
> | **4** Where do you see yourself | **d** attractive in this position? |
> | **5** Can you give me a good reason | **e** your previous experience? |
> | **6** What do you find | **f** of a problem and how you handled it? |
> | **7** What did you learn | **g** in five years' time? |
> | **8** Can you give me an example | **h** from your previous job? |

4 Work in pairs. Think of some suggested answers to the questions in the Professional skills box. Then exchange ideas with another pair. Can you think of any other questions that might be asked during an interview?

5 Work in pairs. Write a list of questions a candidate might want to ask the interviewer. Think about the topics in the box. What topics should a candidate not ask about during an interview?

> career prospects   company hierarchy   company goals   performance appraisal
> previous job holder   scope of the work

Listening

TWO CANDIDATES FOR THE JOB

6))) 8.4   **Listen to Stephen Lang interviewing two candidates for a job as an events and sponsorship manager. Identify the questions from the Professional skills box each candidate was asked. Match the candidates with the questions 1–8.**

Candidate 1: _____
Candidate 2: _____

7)))   **Listen again and answer the questions.**

Which candidate:

1 has a university qualification? ___
2 did a work placement in a sports club? ___
3 needs the job for financial reasons? ___
4 has worked in sales? ___
5 had to solve a problem at work? ___

6 was laid off from his/her previous job? ___
7 thinks he/she is efficient and well-organized? ___
8 enjoys teamwork? ___
9 is interested in the career prospects? ___
10 sounds confident? ___

8 Which of the two candidates do you think is the most likely to be offered the job? Why?

9))) 8.5   **Listen to another candidate and write the questions he asks Stephen Lang.**

1 Could _____?
2 Who _____?

3 What _____?
4 How _____?

10)))   **Can you remember what Stephen Lang's replies to the candidate's questions were? Compare your ideas with a partner. Then listen again and check your answers.**

Speaking

CONDUCTING AN INTERVIEW

11 Work in small groups. Read the advertisement below. Half the group are the interviewers at Wessex Plc and the other half are candidates applying for a job. Roleplay the interview. Then swap roles and repeat the activity.

> Do you speak English? Are you ready to travel?
> Wessex Plc is a UK-based operator with an international network of hotels, resorts and travel companies. As a result of the group's continuing success, we are recruiting personnel to work in a variety of positions from trainee to management level, depending on age, qualifications and experience.
> If you are energetic and ambitious, this is a perfect opportunity to climb the rungs of the career ladder. Training given. Motivating salary for the right people.

Interviewers

- Decide the kind of jobs you are offering and what specific qualifications, experience and skills you require for different posts.
- Prepare a list of questions for the candidates.
- After the interview, decide which candidates you are going to appoint.

Candidates

- Find out what kind of posts are available and decide what you are most interested in.
- Prepare a list of questions for the interviewers.

CASE STUDY
RECRUIT THE RIGHT PERSON

CASE STUDY MENU

Aim: To recruit a new manager for a spa

1 List the qualities needed for the manager of a spa.
2 Listen to people talking about a job profile.
3 Select the best candidate for a post as spa manager.
4 Write a letter of acceptance.

A job profile

1 **Work in pairs. Read the description of the Hygeia spa hotel. Discuss the skills and personal qualities required for a person to be the manager of the spa. Compare your ideas with other people in the class.**

> The Hygeia is a luxury spa hotel offering a wide range of holistic, therapeutic and stress-relieving treatments designed to relax your body and restore a sense of wellbeing. Clients can indulge themselves in the latest hydro-massage, skin and facial treatments in an idyllic setting just a stone's throw from the well-kept beaches of Marbella's Golden Mile.

2))) 8.6 **Listen to three directors of the Hygeia talking about the profile of an assistant manager they wish to recruit and complete the web advertisement.**

> **Job title/Function**
> Assistant Hotel Manager (with spa experience)
>
> **Experience required**
> 3–4 years
>
> **Job description**
> The Asclepius Spa Group is renovating an established spa in Marbella, Spain, with all the facilities of a hotel, aqua gym and spa. The applicant will [1]_____ the day-to-day running of the spa and recruit a team of [2]_____ in wellness treatments. Knowledge of different treatments as well as assistance in the design and marketing of spa services is an advantage but not [3]_____.
>
> **Job requirements**
> • college or university education, preferably higher
> • [4]_____ in Spanish and English strongly [5]_____
> • experience in financial management, keeping [6]_____, ensuring customer satisfaction and [7]_____ staff
> • high level of customer service, excellent communication skills
> • knowledge of the modern spa business and ability to [8]_____ in the market

A short list

3 Work in pairs. You are directors at the Hygeia. You have interviewed a number of candidates and short-listed four of them. Student A, look at the information below. Student B, turn to file 15, page 106. Read the profiles and make notes on the candidates' strengths and weaknesses.

Name: Carlos de Sousa
Age: 32
Nationality: British
Marital status: single
Education: BA (First Class Hons) Economics, Oxford University; MSc in Hospitality and Tourism Management at ISCTE Business School in Lisbon, Portugal
Experience: Worked for six years as a sales engineer promoting a pain-free laser therapy body sculpting procedure, designed to reduce fat and contour the body without invasive surgery. Increased turnover by 25 percent. Five years ago created his own company, de Sousa Consultores. Most recent work has been in providing cost-benefit analyses of the options for restoring spas in a number of European cities.
Languages: bilingual: English/Portuguese
Salary expectations: commensurate with age and experience
Interests: chess, astronomy, fitness
Publications: Recently published a paper entitled *The price sensitivity of Portuguese wellness tourism*, which provided estimates of the effects of fluctuations in the euro's exchange rate.
Interview notes: Highly intelligent and a smooth talker. Said he is looking for a job that is more 'hands-on' and less theoretical. He says he understands Spanish but is not yet fluent. Could he benefit from language training?

Name: Jennifer Watson
Age: 25
Nationality: Australian
Marital status: single
Education: diploma from the Melbourne School of Spa & Hospitality Management.
Experience: After graduating, did a course in aromatherapy and hot stone therapy. Initially employed as a beautician and masseuse in a luxury spa in Sydney, then worked on cruise ships for two years as a fitness instructor and therapist. Subsequently worked in a retail travel agency for one year but got 'bored with selling the same packages to the same kind of customer'. At present works for a major UK tour operator as a holiday rep. She says it's hard work and she has to work long hours but finds it exciting and loves meeting different people all the time.
Languages: native English, school French
Salary expectations: reasonable
Interests: Water skiing, volleyball. Used to be captain of a women's football team. Regularly works out in her local gym.
Interview notes: Attractive personality. Engaged to her Spanish boyfriend. Genuinely enthusiastic about the post but has also been applying for other similar positions. Declared openly at the interview that she wants to combine a career with a family.

TASK

4 Work in groups of four. Discuss the merits and shortcomings of the four candidates in Exercise 3. Decide together which of them you would like to appoint.

5 Work in the same groups. You have just received character references for each of the candidates. Turn to file 16, page 106. Read the references and decide whether or not to maintain your choice.

6 Write a letter of acceptance to the successful candidate. Include the points below in your letter.

- role and responsibilities
- terms and conditions
- duration of probationary period
- acceptance deadline, starting date, duration of contract

UNIT 8: KEY WORDS

autonomous conscientious eligible fringe benefit hands-on headhunt human resources performance-related pay portal reliable supervise time-consuming track record versatile

See DVD-ROM Mini dictionary

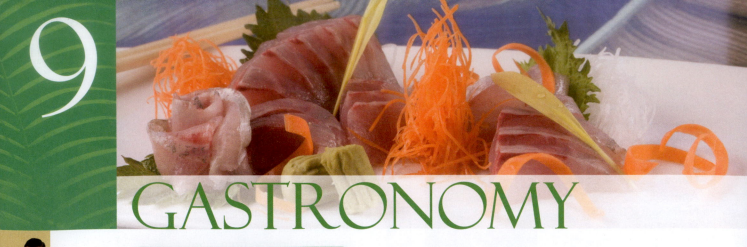

9

GASTRONOMY

UNIT MENU

Grammar: relative clauses

Vocabulary: food and cooking

Professional skills: giving feedback

Case study: Mucho Gusto – plan a new itinerary

Reading

WORLD CUISINE – A QUIZ

1 **How much do you know about world cuisine? Do the quiz and find out.**

> **1** Where did the slow food movement originate?
>   **a** Italy   **b** France   **c** the United States   **d** Senegal
>
> **2** What is fusion cuisine?
>   **a** a mix of sweet and sour sauces in cooking
>   **b** cooking at very low temperatures
>   **c** the application of scientific principles to cooking
>   **d** a cuisine that combines different culinary traditions
>
> **3** Where is the biggest vineyard in the world?
>   **a** Bordeaux, France   **b** California, USA   **c** Piedmont, Italy   **d** Mosel, Germany
>
> **4** Which guidebook awards an annual star rating for restaurants?
>   **a** Dorling Kindersley   **b** Baedeker   **c** Michelin   **d** Lonely Planet
>
> **5** 'Eggplant' is a synonym for which vegetable?
>   **a** aubergine   **b** zucchini   **c** courgette   **d** artichoke
>
> **6** Where do tomatoes originally come from?
>   **a** South America   **b** Southern Europe   **c** North Africa   **d** Polynesia
>
> **7** What kind of dish is a bouillabaisse?
>   **a** an egg-based dessert   **b** a fish stew   **c** a vegetable curry   **d** a type of salad
>
> **8** Which dish of melted cheese and cubes of bread is a national dish of Switzerland?
>   **a** quiche   **b** soufflé   **c** fondue   **d** croque monsieur
>
> **9** Guacamole is an avocado-based dip that originated in which country?
>   **a** Brazil   **b** Panama   **c** Barbados   **d** Mexico
>
> **10** What are the dishes on the left called and what country are they associated with?

2 Work in pairs. Write THREE more quiz questions for your partner to answer.

Listening

AN INTERVIEW WITH JEAN-PIERRE PETIT

3 **))) 9.1**   Listen to an interview with Jean-Pierre Petit, a chef at one of France's most famous restaurants, and check your answers in Exercise 1.

Speaking

LOCAL CUISINE

4 **Discuss the questions with a partner.**

   1 To what extent does food attract tourists to your country or region?

   2 Which dish would you choose to represent your country's culinary culture? Why?

Reading

CULINARY TOURISM

5 **Discuss the questions with a partner. Then read the article and compare your answers with the information in the text.**

   1 What is the difference between eating and dining out?

   2 In what ways can local food benefit the tourist industry?

   3 Think of FIVE reasons why culinary tourism is becoming more popular.

Bon appétit!/Afiyet olsun!/Καλή όρεξη!/Buon appetito!/Приятного аппетита!/Enjoy your meal!

Napoleon once famously said, 'An army marches on its stomach', and so do tourists. A recent study of tourism in the UK found that tourists '**forked out**' more money on food and drink than they did on hotels. Eating is, of course, a necessity, whatever you are doing. But dining out is a pleasure and for a high percentage of tourists the local food and cuisine is an important component of their travel itinerary. The way food is produced, cooked and consumed is part of a country's heritage and the gastronomic tourist seeks to **savour** the 'otherness' of the culinary traditions in the country he or she visits.

The role of food in marketing is increasingly important and destination marketing campaigns around the world demonstrate a strong connection between tourism and gastronomy. Local food holds great potential to enhance sustainability in tourism, maintain a destination's authenticity, strengthen the local economy and provide for an environmentally-friendly infrastructure. In addition, hoteliers and restaurant owners are keen to support local farmers and fishermen, and protect the environment by avoiding **produce** that has been transported long distances.

So what are the trends shaping our interest in culinary tourism? There are possibly five. The first is that tourists are now prepared to spend more of their income on **gourmet products**, dining out and sampling local produce. This is linked to changing demographics and lifestyles; groups such as the affluent 'dinks' (double income no kids), the 'empty nesters' (parents whose children have grown up and left home) and divorcees who take prospective partners out for dinner and away on romantic holidays are all likely candidates for the food tourism market.

A third reason lies in the rejection of **bland** mass-produced food and drink. Tourists are now likely to seek fresh, authentic, good quality cuisine to **tempt the palate**. Gone are the days of the British tourist wanting fish and chips in Ibiza or Americans searching for a fast food chain in Tokyo. Ultimately, the foods that were only consumed abroad end up as standard **fare** in British or American diets – Japanese sushi, Chinese chow mein, Mexican tacos and burritos, Chinese stir-fry and chicken tikka masala are now Britain's favourite dishes. And as foreign foods become more accessible, the tourist interested in gastronomy will be tempted to travel to refine his **palate** and better understand foreign cuisine.

Finally, the role of the media in shaping culinary tourism should not be underestimated. Food programmes presented by celebrity chefs **whet the appetite** of those whose primary purpose is to learn how to cook better. Cooking holidays are a popular niche tourism activity and the number of people enrolling on cookery courses and gastronomic tours in Italy, France, Portugal and Spain has never been higher. You can be sure that it won't be long before the rest of the world invites us to **wine and dine** with them.

---

6 **Match the words in bold in the article in Exercise 5 with the definitions 1–10.**

   1 appeal to the sense of taste _____

   2 having very little taste _____

   3 fully enjoy the taste or smell of food _____

   4 entertain someone with an enjoyable meal _____

   5 the sense of taste, especially the ability to enjoy good food _____

   6 excellent quality food and drink _____

   7 spent _____

   8 increase the desire _____

   9 food that has been grown on a farm to be sold _____

   10 the type of food usually served in a restaurant _____

DESCRIBING DISHES

Reading

SELLING THE MENU

1 Read the advice on increasing restaurant sales and circle the correct options.

How to tempt your customers

To be a really good server, you need to learn the art of tempting your customers. As often as possible, you want your customers to choose the most expensive ¹___ on the menu, as this brings up the average revenue per meal, which pleases the manager and boosts your salary, since your tips are often a percentage of the final ²___. If the customer asks for water, for example, the server should always ask, 'Would you prefer ³___ or sparkling water?' This encourages the customer to buy a bottle of water rather than get it free from the tap. 'What can I get you to drink?' is too open a question and may lead to silence. Much better is a recommendation like 'Can I suggest a freshly-squeezed orange juice or maybe the raspberry lemonade?' Similarly, a question such as 'Would you care for a starter?' can easily end up with a 'No, thank you,' whereas the

same question followed by 'Our chef is doing our ⁴___ favourite tonight: fresh mussels steamed with shallots and served with French fries and a smooth cream and garlic sauce,' makes it sound more appetizing and difficult to refuse. This means that servers should use positive adjectives effectively – words like *smooth, creamy, light, fluffy* and ⁵___. They should talk about the items so the guests can almost taste them as they describe them.

Positive adjectives and foreign words can also be used to enhance the menu, which should always be more than just a list of dishes and prices. 'Salmon with cream, yoghurt, and lemon juice and sliced bread' probably tastes OK but 'Smoked salmon terrine with fresh cream, natural yoghurt and ⁶___ lemon juice served with sliced crusty bread' makes the guest's mouth water.

1 a dishes	**b** tastes	**c** plates	**d** portions
2 a account	**b** bill	**c** invoice	**d** cheque
3 a still	**b** fresh	**c** ordinary	**d** clear
4 a house	**b** kitchen	**c** table	**d** service
5 a cooked	**b** frozen	**c** homemade	**d** raw
6 a acidic	**b** bitter	**c** sour	**d** tangy

2 In what other ways can customers be encouraged to order more than they originally intended? Discuss with a partner.

Vocabulary

DESCRIBING FOOD

3 Put the words in the box in the correct group: positive (P) or negative (N). Then write a short sentence for each.

> appetizing   bland   delicious   done to a turn   greasy   insipid   mouth-watering
> rancid   ripe   rotten   succulent   tasty   tender   tough

4 The verbs in the box all describe ways of cooking food. Which could you use when making a meal with the items 1–6?

> bake   boil   fry   grill   poach   roast   simmer   steam   stew

1 bread   **3** rice   **5** pasta
2 lamb   **4** eggs   **6** potatoes

Listening

DESCRIBING DISHES

5))) **9.2** **Listen to a waiter in a Turkish restaurant describing some dishes to tourists and complete the sentences.**

1

2

3

4

1 Kuzu pirzola are ¹_____ lamb cutlets which are marinated in red pepper, then ²_____ over charcoal and ³_____ with rice.

2 Lahmacun is a kind of Turkish pizza. There's a round bread base that's ⁴_____ in a brick oven and ⁵_____ with minced meat, tomatoes and herbs.

3 Levrek pilaki is a(n) ⁶_____ made by simmering fish with carrots and tomatoes, and ⁷_____ onions and garlic.

4 Midye dolmasi is a delicious dish of ⁸_____ mussels, which are ⁹_____ with a spicy rice mixture, ¹⁰_____ over a low fire and ¹¹_____ by chopped shallots.

GRAMMAR: RELATIVE CLAUSES

1 **Defining relative clauses** define or describe a previous noun or noun phrase. The relative pronoun is either *which*, *that* or *who*.

These are tender baby lamb cutlets **which/that are grilled over charcoal**.

He's the chef **who works in my cousin's restaurant**.

2 In some defining relative clauses the relative pronoun can be omitted.

The dish (that) I ordered was called kuzu pirzola.

3 **Non-defining relative clauses** add non-essential information to the main clause. The relative clause is separated from the main clause by one or two commas. *That* is not used in non-defining relative clauses.

I'm joined by Jean-Pierre Petit, **who is one of France's most famous gourmet chefs**.

Lahmacun, **which is a kind of Turkish pizza**, *is baked on a bread base*.

See Grammar reference, page 115.

6 **Study the Grammar box. Write sentences describing dishes using the prompts. Use defining or non-defining relative clauses.**

1 gazpacho / origin / Andalucía region of Spain / tomato-based soup / served cold

e.g. *Gazpacho, which originated in the Spanish region of Andalucía, is a tomato-based soup usually served cold.*

2 bouillabaisse / traditional fish stew / origin / city of Marseille, France

3 croissants / eaten freshly baked at breakfast / flaky, crescent-shaped pastries

4 pho / Vietnamese noodle soup / served with beef or chicken / popular street food

5 chow mein / popular in American-Chinese cuisine / two main kinds: steamed or crispy / stir-fried dish consisting of noodles, meat and vegetables

6 goulash / origin / Hungary / thick meat stew / popular meal in Eastern Europe

RESEARCH

Visit a local restaurant and take a copy of the menu. Translate the menu into English and describe the dishes using adjectives that make them sound more appealing to a customer. Use the menu in the Writing bank on page 101 to help you.

PROFESSIONAL SKILLS
GIVING FEEDBACK

Listening

CUSTOMER EXPERIENCES

1 What makes a good restaurant? Put the criteria in order of importance for you. Can you think of any others?

a ___ atmosphere **d** ___ food quality **f** ___ service

b ___ background music **e** ___ price **g** ___ wait time

c ___ décor

2))) 9.3 Listen to seven people talking about their recent experiences of eating out. Match the speakers 1–7 with the criteria a–g in Exercise 1.

Reading

ONLINE REVIEWS

3 Read the reviews posted on a travel site about the Chiquita Mexican restaurant and list the problems the diners encountered.

1

13 August
If you want service, this place is not for you. We sat down at a table and waited and waited … Finally, a waiter (no pun intended!) appeared out of nowhere. I ordered a salad with grilled shrimp with the dressing on the side and, of course, it came with the dressing on it. Also, the shrimps were not grilled as I'd asked – they were sautéed. The grand finale: since the club soda I'd asked for was obviously flat, I decided to try and get a glass of sparkling water with a slice of lemon. I mean, how could that get messed up? She comes back, still water, no lemon.

2

14 August
It was completely disorganized. I was with a large group of people and it took over an hour for most of them to get their food. I noticed they were asking other people at different tables what their orders were again.

3

15 August
The first thing that you will notice, which ended up getting on our nerves, is the loud music – so loud that at times we could hardly hear each other speak. The second thing you will notice is the great choice of dishes. And my T-bone steak was done to a turn.

4

16 August
I know the waitress depends on tips for her wages but I find it annoying when servers come up to you every five minutes and ask you if you're enjoying your meal. If it was OK five minutes ago, why ask again? And if I'm in the middle of a conversation, I don't like being interrupted and asked how I'm doing. This said, she was doing her best and I must say the food was delicious.

5

17 August
I ordered the chimichanga, rice and beans 'garnished with guacamole and sour cream'. But there was no garnish and when I complained, the waiter said they had run out of guacamole. How can a Mexican restaurant run out of guacamole?

6

18 August
I don't know if this restaurant has a dishwasher or they wash up by hand but my plate still had some dried brown stuff on it and the cutlery was greasy.

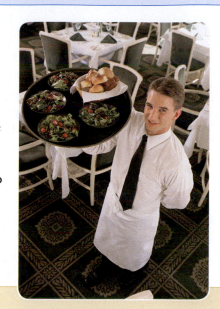

Listening

GIVING FEEDBACK

4)))9.4 Listen to the manager of the Chiquita talking to his staff and identify the problems he raises and the proposed solutions.

5 Which TWO problems from the reviews did the manager forget to speak about? What could he have said to the staff about them?

6 Complete the Professional skills box. Match the advice on giving feedback to staff 1–6 with the headings a–f.

PROFESSIONAL SKILLS: GIVING FEEDBACK

1 ___
Usually feedback should be relayed at regular intervals. Don't wait for the next scheduled appraisal if something important needs to be said right now.

2 ___
Staff will generally receive negative comments more readily if they are mixed with sincere praise for other things.

3 ___
Make it clear that you're talking about specific actions that could be improved, not criticizing your listener's character.

4 ___
Listen attentively to what the other person has to say. Don't assume you know why a mistake has been made. Ask questions. (e.g. *On a scale of 1–10, how would you rate the service? What went wrong? How do you think you could have handled this better?*)

5 ___
Make sure that you channel the conversation towards ways so that your listener can make progress. Feedback should always be accompanied by recommendations for improvement.

6 ___
Tell your staff what they've done right or well and why it was right. Next, give them the bad news: why it is unsatisfactory and what to do about it. Then end on an upbeat note. The end of a conversation greatly influences the way people react to it.

a Create a dialogue.
b Choose the right time.
c Put forward solutions.
d Use the feedback sandwich.
e Include positive feedback.
f Focus on the problem, not the person.

Speaking

DEALING WITH CUSTOMER FEEDBACK

7 Work in pairs. Student A, turn to file 17, page 107. Student B, turn to file 27, page 110. Roleplay a feedback session between the manager of the East Quay restaurant and a server. Follow the advice in the Professional skills box.

Writing

RESTAURANT REVIEW

8 Write a review (150–200 words) for a travel magazine about a meal you recently had in a restaurant. Mention all the criteria in Exercise 1.

RESEARCH

What other problems may diners encounter in a restaurant? Search the internet for problems/reviews that people have posted.

CASE STUDY
PLAN A NEW ITINERARY

CASE STUDY MENU

Aim: To plan a new itinerary for a gastronomic tour.

1 Listen to an interview about creating a gastronomic tour.

2 Read the itinerary of a gastronomic tour.

3 Read comments posted on a travel forum.

4 Plan a new itinerary.

A gastronomic tour of Peru

PERU

1))) 9.5 **Listen to an interview with Rosa Huanca about her experience of creating a gastronomic tour in Peru and answer the questions.**

1 What do the numbers 650,000, 100,000 and 2,000 represent?

2 Why does she mention potatoes and quinoa, and olives and grapes?

3 What does the Peruvian dish called papa a la huancaína consist of and why is it significant?

4 What are chifas, tiradito and ceviche? What is their link with the Japanese and Chinese immigrant communities in Peru?

Tour itinerary

2 **Read the itinerary of Mucho Gusto, the gastronomic tour created by Rosa Huanca, and answer the questions.**

1 In your opinion, how 'complete' is this culinary tour?

2 What is the high point of the tour?

Mucho Gusto is a complete culinary tour blending together the flavour of native, creole and fusion foods. Experience the exotic tastes and ingredients of the Mistura food festival, take part in a cookery class to try traditional recipes and crown your stay with a visit to the magical Machu Picchu.

• **Day 1:** arrival in Lima; overnight accommodation in budget hotel

• **Day 2:** breakfast on acaldo de gallino (hen soup), known as the soup 'levanta muertos', a dish to 'wake the dead'; visit to a local market to purchase ingredients for tomorrow's cookery class; dinner at the Costanera 700 restaurant to experience the Japanese and Asian influence in Peruvian cuisine

• **Day 3:** introduction to Peruvian cuisine; learn how to prepare Peru's staple dishes and afterwards taste the many dishes you made during class

• **Day 4:** early morning flight to Cuzco by AeroCondor, followed by a spectacular four-hour train journey through rolling hills and picturesque villages to Machu Picchu, the sacred valley of the Incas

• **Day 5:** overnight stay in Cuzco at the Casa San Blas Boutique Hotel; gourmet lunch at the Cicciolina; return to Lima and hotel

• **Day 6:** Mistura food festival; attend demonstrations and taste exquisite dishes from the country's top restaurants and chefs

• **Day 7:** shopping in Lima and return flight

Customer feedback

3 Rosa is now preparing a tour for her second year of activity. Work in pairs. Student A, look at the information below. Student B, turn to file 18, page 107. Read the comments Rosa received and make a list of the main complaints and suggestions.

The stay got off to a bad start: no driver at the airport to take us to our hotel. Two hours and 15 minutes later – and many phone calls, at our expense – he finally turned up. He seemed not to know the way to the hotel, which, in my opinion, was pretty substandard. The 'early morning flight' on Day 4 turned out to be at 5:30 a.m. but the flight was delayed and by the time we arrived, it was well into the afternoon. We had hardly arrived when we had to go back!

I never expected to get food poisoning from a gourmet lunch! From the menu I chose the main courses aij de gallina (chicken) and the savoury beef, and as dessert the volador y guargueros (egg-based pastry). Although the service and taste of the food was OK, I was violently sick from it and felt terrible during the next two days. Looking at it now, I assume that I got salmonella from the dessert because it contained milk and eggs. Given the fact that this establishment tries to come across as a high-end restaurant for trusted food, this is absolutely not the case and I would recommend you drop this from the itinerary.

The toilets were interesting in the hotels we stayed at. They didn't have toilet seats, so be prepared to squat, hover or fall in AND bring your own toilet paper! Away from the city, on the Inca Trail, prepare for the worst. I think you should point this out to all travellers beforehand.

I was really impressed by the day at the Mistura. As well as sampling the local specialities, I had the opportunity to speak to members of the various indigenous communities, who told me about the richness of their country, their happiness at being part of the 'Peruvian food revolution' and about their sense of national pride at having their food on show. The festival left a powerful and unforgettable impression on me. But it lasts for ten days! Why did we have to leave so early?

4 🔊 **9.6** Rosa is changing her programme to take account of the feedback. She has gone into partnership with Luis Calderón, who has experience in organizing similar tours. Listen to their conversation. What changes do they suggest a) to the culinary experience and b) to other activities?

TASK

5 Work in small groups. You are going to plan what Rosa and Luis should offer for next year's gastronomic tour. Follow the steps below.

1 Brainstorm your ideas. Think about the length of the tour, the type of activities and practical information such as transport and accommodation.

2 Rewrite the website itinerary from Exercise 2, describing the tour and its activities. Include a section on relevant practical information. There is space for 400 words on the website.

UNIT 9: KEY WORDS

bake   bland   celebrity chef   dine out
done to a turn   fare   fusion cuisine
mouth-watering   oven   savour   simmer
speciality (BrE)/specialty (AmE)   staple   stew
whet the appetite

See DVD-ROM Mini dictionary

10

RISK

UNIT MENU

Grammar: modal verbs

Vocabulary: disasters, adventure sports

Professional skills: dealing with crises

Game: the Olympic Game

Reading

MINIMIZING RISK

1 **Read the advice given by a hotel manager and a restaurant chef on avoiding accidents in the workplace. Complete the table. Which workplace would you consider the riskiest?**

	Type of risk	Measures taken
hotel		
restaurant		

One of the most important aspects of running a hotel is minimizing the various risks associated with this type of business. The greatest potential area of exposure is the property itself. Fire is a constant hazard, so proper maintenance of all the electrical wiring and heating systems must be a top priority in order to anticipate and mitigate the risk. Here we've installed smoke alarms, fire extinguishers and sprinklers in all the key areas to limit the damage if a fire does break out. Of course, smoking is not permitted in any part of the building. And the high-rise hotel I manage poses a particular problem evacuating the building in the event of a fire alert, so all the exits are clearly indicated and any obstructions can be quickly removed. There's also an emergency lighting system if there is a power failure.

Kitchens are potentially hazardous places, so we try to foresee the risks involved in food preparation and take measures to prevent any serious injuries. With many electrical appliances, there is a constant threat of electrocution because water spillages and grease fires increase the dangers caused by electricity. So, we tell our staff not to plug anything in if the cord is wet or if they're touching a wet surface. All our sockets have a built-in circuit breaker which stops the flow of electricity before a dangerous amount passes through a person's body. And because a kitchen is a wet place, many of the accidents in the catering industry are caused by people slipping on wet floors. We have extraction and ventilator fans to remove steam and grease before it can be deposited on the floor and work surfaces. All our staff are trained to use lids on pans, especially when they are being carried. Any spillages must be wiped up immediately and any leakages, for example, a dishwasher, must be reported straightaway. And to avoid people tripping up or slipping, we issue sensible non-slip shoes to kitchen staff. Sandals or open-top shoes are not allowed.

Speaking

POTENTIAL RISKS IN HOTELS AND RESTAURANTS

2 **Look at some potential risks in hotels and restaurants. How can these risks be reduced? Discuss with a partner.**

1 hotels: theft, intruders, swimming pools, storm damage

2 restaurants: food poisoning, sharp knives, skin infections, hot surfaces

Vocabulary

TYPES OF RISK

3 **Put the words in the box in the correct group. Then add at least one word to each group.**

> avalanches   currency fluctuations   demonstrations   floods   fraud   hijacking
> hurricanes   infectious diseases   kidnapping   pandemics   personal injuries
> recession   riots   rising fuel prices   strikes

Types of risk				
Natural	Health	Economic	Civil unrest	Crime

RISK PREVENTION

4 **Circle the word in italics that has a different meaning from the others.**

1 We do everything possible to *minimize / mitigate / limit / spread* the risk.

2 It's not always possible to *anticipate / foresee / monitor / predict* the risk.

3 We've taken steps to *avert / avoid / prevent / warn* the risk.

4 A restaurant kitchen is quite a *dangerous / hazardous / protected / treacherous* place.

5 Open-top shoes are not *allowed / authorized / enabled / permitted* in the kitchen.

Listening

BEST PRACTICE IN RISK MANAGEMENT

5 **))) 10.1** **Lisa Richards is the director of a major tour operator. Listen to her talking about best practice in risk management and identify the points below.**

• possible sources of risk

• four stages of risk management

• who is involved

6 **)))** **Complete the sentences from the recording with the words in the box. Then listen again and check your answers.**

> address   brainstorm   consult   monitor   prioritize   review

1 The first stage is to identify the source of risk, and the nature and scope of issues that we need to ¹_____ in order to ensure the safety of the destination.

2 So, we have to be proactive, ²_____ all the risks that we can possibly think of and ³_____ them in order of importance.

3 We also ⁴_____ representatives from all the key stakeholders in the local community.

4 It is important to ⁵_____ and ⁶_____ the risk management plan on a regular basis.

EXTREME SPORTS

Speaking

ADVENTURE SPORTS

1 Work in pairs. Put the adjectives in the box in order of risk from lowest (1) to highest (5).

> acceptable   considerable   huge   remote   slight

2 Put the adventure sports in the box in order from the most (1) to the least dangerous (8). Then justify your choices to a partner.

> bungee jumping   horseback riding   hot-air ballooning   mountaineering
> potholing   skiing   skydiving   whitewater rafting

3 Choose two of the sports in Exercise 2 and carry out a risk assessment. List the things that could go wrong.

4 What precautions could adventure sports organizers take to ensure safety? Discuss with a partner. Consider the issues in the box and any others you can think of.

> equipment   information to the public   rescue procedures   training

Listening

BREAKING NEWS

5))) 10.2   Listen to a news report about an accident at a ski resort and answer the questions.

1 How many people were involved? Who were they?

2 What happened exactly?

3 Whose fault was it, according to the report?

Reading

DRAMA AT BEAVER RIDGE

6 **Read a web article about the accident in Exercise 5 and some readers' comments. Discuss the questions with a partner.**

1 The web article and the radio broadcast in Exercise 5 relate the same event but the radio broadcast contains four mistakes of fact. What are they?

2 How could the accident have been avoided?

3 Who do you think was to blame?

> A young girl was seriously injured yesterday by a snow groomer at Beaver Ridge.
>
> The accident occurred at 6.19 p.m. after the closure of the ski resort, when the girl sliding down a beginner slope with her twin brother on a round plastic sled hit the machine. Her brother was luckily able to throw himself off the sled before the impact.
>
> The groomer's driver was in a state of shock last night after having been released by the police. 'He's a very experienced driver and must have been driving slowly at the time – no more than nine kilometres an hour. He couldn't possibly have seen the sled,' said the director of the resort. 'People shouldn't be on the slopes once the pistes have closed for the day.'
>
> One of the ski instructors, who did not wish to be named, said, 'The slopes are invaded every day after six o'clock by children and their sleds. No one has ever stopped them, so I've always assumed it's tolerated.'

> 'The resort should have put up a notice: *No sleds or snowboards after closure*. People shouldn't have been on the slopes at that time of day.'

> 'Disagree. There's a Beaver Ridge bylaw that says that the ski resort cannot be held liable after the slopes have closed. The kids play there at their own risk and, in my opinion, the accident is the fault of the parents, who should have been with their children at all times.'

> 'The resort owes a "duty of care" to all users and is legally obliged to foresee all the dangers. The resort was obviously in breach of that duty and the owners should have informed users of the hazard.'

7 **Study the Grammar box. Which sentences indicate:**

1 something that is possible but not certain?

2 something the speaker thinks is certain?

3 a criticism?

8 **Write sentences speculating about the causes of the accidents below and indicating any failures or omissions. Use the modal verbs in the Grammar box.**

1 A woman was knocked over while she was speaking with her ski instructor. The skier, a man who was on the slope for the first time, no doubt saw her but was out of control. He had also come through an area that was off limits. He denied responsibility and also provided incorrect contact details after the accident.

2 The owner of a whitewater rafting operation was approached by a manufacturer to test a new design of raft. A child drowned when it capsized and the family sued for negligence. The owner's insurance policy had run out two months previously and hadn't been renewed.

GRAMMAR: MODAL VERBS

Use a modal verb + *have* + past participle (+ *-ing*) to speculate about the past or express criticism. Different verbs show different degrees of certainty.

The driver **may/might have been** taken ill.

He **couldn't** possibly **have seen** the sled.

He **must have been driving** very slowly at the time.

The owners **should have informed** users of the hazard.

People **shouldn't have been** on the slopes at that time.

See Grammar reference, page 115.

3 A novice skier was seriously injured after colliding with a tree. The man was with a group of other skiers who were stuck on the mountainside due to bad weather when the accident happened. Their ski instructor had told them to ski off-piste down the slopes. Weather warnings had been issued and the ski parties had been advised to return immediately. The instructor said he was 'pretty sure' he did not hear the forecast. The organizers of the package denied responsibility, maintaining that the weather was an act of God and beyond their control.

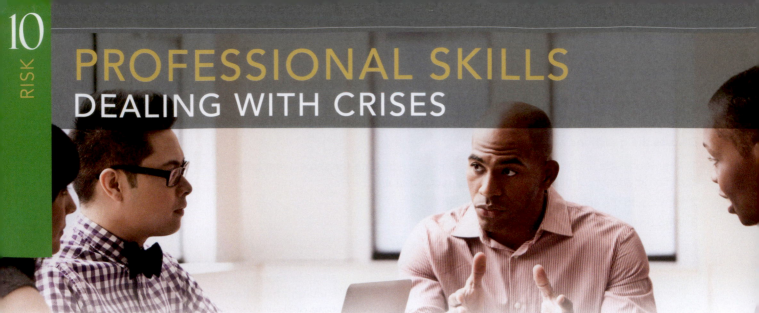

PROFESSIONAL SKILLS
DEALING WITH CRISES

Listening

CRISIS MANAGEMENT PLAN

1))) **10.3** **Listen to a conversation between a group of tour operators. Are the statements true (T) or false (F)? Correct the false statements.**

1 Most companies have a crisis management plan. T / F

2 A villa holiday is less risky than an adventure holiday. T / F

3 The first hour in a crisis is the most critical. T / F

4 Most companies can easily contact relatives in an emergency. T / F

5 Social networking sites are an excellent channel of communication in a crisis. T / F

2))) **Listen again. What advice do the speakers give to companies to prepare them to cope with an emergency?**

3 **Look at the crisis management plan in the Professional skills box and put the steps in the correct group. Which THREE steps do you think are the most important things to do?**

Before the crisis	During the crisis	After the crisis

PROFESSIONAL SKILLS: DEALING WITH CRISES

1 Produce an immediate plan of action that prioritizes needs and is based on an accurate assessment of the emergency situation.

2 Provide prompt and effective action to prevent escalation of the situation.

3 Prepare your organization's contingency plans for handling emergency situations.

4 Identify the types of records that must be completed in the event of an emergency and how to complete and submit them.

5 Work out an action plan to make sure the disaster does not happen again.

6 Develop a media communications strategy in the event of a major crisis.

7 Conduct a post-crisis review to learn the lessons of the past.

8 Set up a hotline to keep relatives and friends adequately informed.

9 Anticipate every imaginable situation that might arise, man-made or natural, starting with those that are most likely to happen.

Reading

FACING THE MEDIA

4 Read the guidelines for facing press and television journalists. Complete them with phrases a–f.

a we are committed to providing

b we understand seven people were taken to hospital

c we are extremely concerned

d information is not yet at our disposal

e the situation is being investigated further

f we will, of course, do everything in our power

Briefing the media

Preparing information to use when facing the media during a crisis can be the most difficult aspect of crisis management. Here are some handy tips.

- Be quick to relay the information at your disposal but do not speculate. If details are not available, say, 'Complete ¹___ but ²___ by the proper authorities.'

- Deal with the facts of the situation and express your concern. For example, 'We learnt of the coach crash this morning and ³___ whenever we hear about any accident. According to our information, everyone has been taken by ambulance to the nearest hospital. On behalf of the company, I would like to send our best wishes for a speedy recovery to those who were injured and ⁴___ to keep next of kin informed of any developments.'

- If there is a transport accident, point out that such accidents are rare. 'Our overall safety record is very solid. This has never happened on one of our tours before and ⁵___ the safest holiday possible.'

- If a natural disaster such as a flood or tornado occurs, state the facts relating to the location and casualties, as well as the history of such disasters. 'The storm reached hurricane strength at 4.30 in the morning and ⁶___ suffering from shock when the hotel roof was blown away. This is the first time the area has known a storm of this magnitude.'

- If you are asked what you intend to do to protect travellers, inform them of all the measures you currently take to ensure the safety of your passengers or visitors. Follow up with any additional future plans you intend to put in place.

Speaking

INTERVIEW ROLEPLAY

5 Work in pairs. Student A, turn to file 19, page 107. You are the local representative of a tour operator. One of your biggest hotels in Southeast Asia has been hit by a typhoon and flooded. **Student B, turn to file 28, page 110.** You are a journalist. Roleplay the interview.

RESEARCH

Find out about some of the crises that have affected tourist destinations (e.g. New York, 9/11/2001; SARS virus, Asia-Pacific region, 2003; Indian Ocean tsunami, 2004; Hurricane Katrina, 2005, New Orleans; Fukushima tsunami, 2011; Hurricane Sandy, 2012, eastern US).

- What was the nature of the crisis?
- What had been done to avoid the scenario?
- What measures were taken during and immediately after the disaster?
- To what extent has the risk of another crisis been mitigated?

Present your findings to the class.

THE OLYMPIC GAME

START

1 →

Your capital city has been chosen for the next Olympic Games. Congratulations!

2 →

A journalist asks you what the short-term benefits and drawbacks are likely to be in terms of increased visitor numbers.

3 →

As director of tourism operations in the capital city, you are asked what kind of infrastructure and new installations will be needed to cope with the influx of visitors.

4 →

The government has just increased t rate of VAT and airport fees. A journ asks you if this will risk a decline in v numbers despite the Olympics.

FINISH

24

The closing ceremony is broadcast to over 20 billion people. Hold a round-table discussion to talk about the long-term benefits of the games.

23

A journalist says that any net increase in leisure tourism after the games risks being very limited. What is your opinion?
←

21

Go back three spaces.
→

22 ↑

There are complaints from visitors that too few tickets are available to members of the public as many have gone to institutional sponsors. What is your reaction?

20 ↑

A TV news item includes interviews with foreign visitors who have been victims of overbooking. A journalist asks you for your opinion.

19

Many hotels have not been refurbished to help people with disabilities in advance of the Paralympics. What more needs to be done?
←

18
←

?

17

You are asked what kind of risk assessment procedures you have carried out at your hotel in advance of the Olympics.
←

1))) 10.4 **Listen to an interview with a member of the organizing committee for the Olympic Games talking about the benefits of the forthcoming games to the host nation. Number the benefits in the order you hear them.**

a employment ___

b patriotism ___

c inbound tourism ___

d international reputation ___

e sports facilities ___

f urban renewal ___

2 **Work in groups of three or four. Follow the instructions and play the game.**

Instructions

1 Toss a coin to move. Heads = move one square. Tails = move two squares.

2 Read the question or situation on each square to another member of the group. He/She has to speak about the topic for one minute, without hesitation or repetition. If he/she speaks successfully for one minute, he/she moves forward one square. If he/she speaks for two minutes, he/she moves forward two squares.

3 If a player lands on a square with a question mark, he/she can choose his/her own topic (related to the Olympic Games) to talk about for one minute.

4 All the other members of the group help to decide if the player speaking is successful or not but the person who read the question makes the final decision.

5 The first person to reach 'Finish' is the winner.

5 →
A recent report suggests that much improvement is needed in the service and quality of hotels and restaurants in the capital. What are your solutions?

6 →
A journalist asks you how the risk of a terrorist attack during the games is being dealt with.

7 →
Many international visitors risk staying for a short period and neglecting other parts of the country. What plans are there to encourage people to visit sites away from the capital?

8 ↓
?

10
High visa costs and difficulty completing visa forms is deterring visitors from important countries like China and India. What are your solutions?
↓

9
A journalist asks you what measures will be taken to deal with the inevitable rise in street crime during the Olympics.
←

11 →
The city's main airport is experiencing long delays in processing people through immigration. Go back three spaces and tell a journalist what your solutions are.

12 ↓
?

16
Millions of tourists, many from countries where a pandemic is likely to emerge, may create a health hazard. What strategy has been put in place to anticipate the outbreak of disease?
←

15
A threatened transport strike risks causing chaos on the road and rail network. Go back three spaces and tell a journalist what your contingency plans are.
←

14
People are saying the city will be overcrowded and hotel prices exorbitant. As a result, visitor numbers could actually go down. What is your reaction?
←

13
The area chosen for the new stadium is well away from the core tourist areas. A journalist asks if there are plans to invest in new hotel accommodation.
←

UNIT 10: KEY WORDS

civil unrest   electrocution   emergency
evacuate   extinguisher   hazard
infection   maintenance   mitigate
negligence   poisoning   potholing
slipping   spillage   trip
See DVD-ROM Mini dictionary

A World Heritage site

1 Complete the text about Bridgetown, a World Heritage site, with the words in the box.

> comprises   consists   dates back   elegant   insight   located

> ¹_____ on the Caribbean island of Barbados, historic Bridgetown is an outstanding example of British colonial architecture and ²_____ of a well-preserved old town that ³_____ to the 17th century. The property also ⁴_____ a nearby military garrison with numerous ⁵_____ historic buildings. With its serpentine street layout, the property gives a unique and detailed ⁶_____ into British colonial town planning, compared to the Spanish and Dutch colonial cities in the region, which were arranged in the form of a grid.

Architectural features

2 Match the words 1–8 with the definitions a–h.

1 chandelier	**a** the rooms occupied by servants as part of their job
2 mantelpiece	**b** a type of sculpture in which shapes are cut from the surrounding stone
3 quarters	**c** a rounded roof on a building or a room
4 spire	**d** a floor consisting of small flat blocks of wood fitted together in a pattern
5 dome	**e** a covered passage with arches or pillars along the outer side
6 bas-relief	**f** a decorative light with several branches that hangs from the ceiling
7 parquet	**g** a tall pointed structure on top of a building
8 arcade	**h** a shelf above a fireplace

Tour guiding

3 Complete the extract from a guided tour with the words in the box.

> carved   colonnades   depicts   ornate   restored   sweeping   vaulted   wing

> We're now standing in the main entrance hall and if you look up, you can admire the
> [1]_____ ceiling, which is painted in the rococo style, and [2]_____ a series of allegorical
> scenes. To your left is the vast [3]_____ marble staircase designed by Gasparini, which
> was severely damaged by fire in the 19th century but subsequently [4]_____ according to
> the original designs. Along the walls is a series of slender
> [5]_____ elaborately embellished with [6]_____ patterns in the Baroque style of the 18th
> century. In the antechamber leading to the west [7]_____ you'll see a statue of the
> Queen [8]_____ from a single block of marble. In a minute we'll make our way to the
> throne room and the royal chambers.

Talking about the past

4 Rewrite the sentences using the words in brackets.

1 The area around St Petersburg was originally a marshy swamp. (used)

2 In 17th-century London merchants often discussed business in one of the new coffee houses. (would)

3 Historians were previously of the opinion that the Egyptian pharaoh Ramses III was poisoned. (believe)

4 They now think that Ramses III was assassinated by his wife and son. (it)

5 There is some evidence that the Viking explorer Erik the Red reached North America 500 years before Christopher Columbus. (said)

Hypothetical situations

5 Write a sentence beginning with *if* for each situation.

1 I was able to make the booking for you because someone cancelled at the last minute.

   e.g. *If someone hadn't cancelled at the last minute, I wouldn't have been able to make the booking for you.*

2 Everyone could hear her presentation because she was wearing a microphone.

3 The match was called off because the pitch was frozen.

4 I didn't know the projector wasn't working, which explains why I didn't call a technician.

5 The festival was such a great success because we invited the most popular bands.

6 We didn't have a generous sponsor, so we lost a lot of money.

Contracts

6 Complete the extract from a contract with the words in the box.

> assign   in writing   null and void   prior   provisions
> shall apply   shall be construed   shall be liable

> The present Agreement sets out the terms and
> conditions which [1]_____ to the services and goods
> carried out or provided by the Event Planner. The
> purchaser [2]_____ for all costs and expenses, including
> insurance and delivery. Any contrary terms or conditions
> stipulated at whatever moment in time by the purchaser
> shall, unless expressly authorized, be [3]_____.
>   Neither party shall have the right to [4]_____ any of its
> rights or obligations under this Agreement to any other
> company, firm or person without obtaining the
> [5]_____ consent and approval [6]_____ of the other party.
> The [7]_____ of this Agreement [8]_____ in accordance with
> the laws of the United Arab Emirates.

Event concept

7 Circle the correct options in italics.

1 We expect at least 2,000 people to *attend / put on / stage* the conference in November.

2 We were obliged to *put out / put off / put down* the event until the next day because of the bad weather.

3 Sellebrations is an events management company that can *call off / cater for / draw up* any special occasion.

4 Our head office will *liaise / sponsor / programme* with the suppliers to ensure deliveries are made on time.

5 The main aim of the exhibition is to *hold / put on / showcase* tourist destinations in the UK.

Dependent prepositions

8 Complete the sentences with prepositions.

1 Are you interested ¹_____ applying ²_____ the job?

2 After a couple of years you should be eligible ³_____ promotion.

3 He has a previous track record ⁴_____ spa management and we could benefit ⁵_____ his experience.

4 She takes great pride ⁶_____ her work and is a great benefit ⁷_____ the firm.

5 I don't object ⁸_____ a handwritten covering letter but I see little point ⁹_____ not typing it.

6 You'll soon become familiar ¹⁰_____ our procedures – it's just a question ¹¹_____ time.

Job interviews

9 Match the questions 1–6 with the answers a–f.

1 What do you seek from a job?

2 Would you be willing to relocate?

3 What do you consider are your greatest strengths?

4 What is your main weakness?

5 What have you learnt from any failures?

6 Why do you want to join our company?

a To analyse myself, find out any shortcomings and identify areas for improvement.

b It has one of the fastest growth rates in the industry and that would mean a faster growth rate for me as a professional.

c A challenging role and an opportunity to use my skills and progress.

d Maybe I'm a bit stubborn. I'm a perfectionist and I don't like to settle for second best.

e I'm versatile and resourceful, so I think I can handle any type of people and situation.

f I'm mobile and can go to any part of the country or abroad if the situation requires it.

Personal qualities

10 Read the definitions and complete the adjectives.

1 able to work on one's own   a _ t _ n o _ _ u _

2 sociable and interested in others   o _ _ g _ i _ g

3 doing things carefully, using an ordered system m _ _ h _ d _ c _ l

4 determined to be successful   a m _ _ t _ _ u _

5 able to talk easily and effectively   a _ t i _ _ l _ t _

6 that can be trusted and depended on r _ l _ _ b _ e

Describing dishes

11 Match the adjectives 1–7 with the foods a–g.

1 mild   a butter

2 greasy   b curry

3 sour   c French fries

4 rancid   d lemon

5 sweet and sour e peach

6 tender   f sauce

7 ripe   g steak

Culinary tourism

12 Complete the text about a culinary holiday with the words in the box.

> dine out   fare   gourmet
> palate   produce   savouring
> slow food   whet

From a gastronomic point of view, Piedmont is undoubtedly one of Italy's most interesting regions. The food produced there will please your eye and tempt your ¹_____. There is an enormous choice of dishes, ranging from traditional country ²_____ to creatively modern cuisine. Moreover, the region is the centre of the ³_____ revolution that is transforming the art of cooking in Italy and beyond.

For our upcoming tour, we will be spending time in the countryside, visiting farmers' markets and ⁴_____ the local agricultural ⁵_____ in order to ⁶_____ your appetite before learning how to cook Italian-style with our resident chef Paolo Palermo. There will also be plenty of opportunities to ⁷_____ in some of the region's superb restaurants, from simple rustic trattorias, to Michelin-starred, ⁸_____ establishments, all serving some of Italy's finest food.

Modal verbs

13 Read the newspaper article and complete the sentences. Use the verbs in the box and *could*, *might*, *should* or *must*.

Bungee jumper's miraculous survival

A 21-year-old girl on an adventure holiday in Africa was in a state of shock last night after the rubber cord broke during her bungee jump from a bridge above a crocodile-infested river. She miraculously survived the 35-metre fall and escaped with severe bruising, a broken collarbone and suspected internal injuries.

The bungee operator was apparently using the same rubber cord that had snapped in a previous incident at another site. No safety checks had been carried out and there were no personnel on the river bank.

Interviewed in hospital, she said, 'I was able to swim to the shore but when I was pulled out of the water by passers-by, they laid me on my back instead of on my side and I was choking on the water I'd inhaled.'

Contacted by telephone, the operator stated a member of staff with first aid training and the necessary recovery equipment will now be posted below the bridge at all times.

> be   carry out   ~~eat~~   have   lay   post   suffer   use

1 She was very lucky as she *could have been eaten* by crocodiles.

2 She _____ internal injuries.

3 She _____ much more seriously injured.

4 The bungee operator _____ the same rubber cord involved in another accident.

5 The operator _____ safety checks on a daily basis.

6 The passers-by _____ her on her side and not on her back.

7 A qualified person _____ below the bridge on the river bank.

8 She _____ the fright of her life!

Reports

> Reports should be organized clearly and in a logical order and written in formal or neutral language. Most reports should contain:
>
> - a title page
> - an executive summary (gives an overview of the contents of the report)
> - an introduction (outlines the main points to be discussed)
> - findings (presents and discusses what the research has uncovered)
> - a conclusion (synthesizes the findings and interprets them)
> - recommendations (makes practical suggestions for the future)
> - appendices (extra relevant documents that the reader can consult)

The Morris report: patterns in booking, transport and destination preferences in Europe

1 Executive summary

The Morris Institute of Tourism Research conducted a survey into attitudes to tourism in order to determine changing patterns in booking, transport and destination preferences among a sample of European countries. The goal was to enable tourism providers to gain a better understanding of visitor profiles and their aspirations.

2 Introduction

The survey was carried out by telephone over a period of three months in selected EU countries. The objective was to study people's motivations for going on holiday, how they researched their holiday prior to departure, their preferred destinations and activities and any reasons why they had not taken a holiday in the previous year.

3 Findings

3.1 Almost half (46%) of the respondents who went away for at least five nights did so for rest and recreation, while just under a third (31%) stayed with friends and relatives.

3.2 The most important factor in the choice of destination was the location's natural features, such as the climate and geography, while 29% cited the quality of accommodation. Many (57%) relied on recommendations from friends and colleagues, and a small minority (7%) used social networks or consulted sites such as TripAdvisor. 54% used the internet to book their holiday, an increase of 6% over the previous year.

3.3 A large majority (66%) of respondents had their holiday in their own country. Spain was the most visited EU country, followed by Italy and France.

One in four said they went on holiday for the sun or the beach. For one in five respondents, nature tourism was the main interest, a slightly higher proportion than city breaks (17%). Other motivations included exploring the cultural heritage, with a minority going for sports activities such as kayaking or windsurfing.

3.4 Those who had not been on holiday during the current year cited financial reasons (the vast majority), pressure of work and lack of time. Just under a quarter of respondents said that they had decided not to go away for personal or private reasons, without specifying what these reasons were.

4 Conclusion

It is clear that for reasons of economy more people are choosing to stay in their own country or travel relatively short distances. The number of respondents who stay with family and friends rather than in paid accommodation also reflects the financial pressures.

An important trend highlighted by the survey is the increasing importance of the internet to travel planning. Many more people used the web to arrange their holidays than travel agents, while websites were second only to personal recommendations for researching holidays.

5 Recommendations

Socio-demographic data needs to be collected on a regular basis in order to target different client profiles in different countries. For example, Spain was the most popular holiday destination for the Irish (31%), the Norwegians (21%), the Portuguese (20%) and the British (19%). Marketing campaigns should therefore take into account local preferences.

Meeting minutes

There is no single specific format for writing minutes that you need to follow. However, the minutes of a meeting should always answer the following questions:

- When was the meeting?
- Who was present?
- Who did not attend? (Include this information if it matters.)
- What topics were discussed?
- What decisions were taken?
- What actions were agreed upon?
- Who is to implement the decisions and by when?
- When and where is the next meeting?

It is a good idea to write up the minutes as soon as possible after the meeting, while the discussions are still fresh in your mind. Follow the order of the agenda and use a numbering system.

Write minutes using reported speech but don't provide a long narrative; record the topics discussed, the decisions made and action points. Action points and decisions need to be made clear for future reference. You can write in the active voice if you want to identify a person specifically and what they said (e.g. *Gabriella confirmed that counter staff needed more training.*). For more formal contexts, or if you do not want to identify who said what, you can use the passive voice (e.g. *Concern was expressed about customer service standards.*).

Tourism Committee meeting of 8 May 20__

Present: Richard Keller, Karen Anderson, Jodi Ruzicka, Larry Wiedemann, Jerry Lucas
Apologies for absence: Vera Mathews

Chairman Richard Keller called the meeting to order at 2.30 p.m.

1   The minutes of the 7 April meeting were read and approved.
2   Jodi Ruzicka presented a grant request of $38,000 for an extension to the Visitor Information Bureau at Sandy Point. Jerry Lucas pointed out that this sum seemed excessive and that the Bureau had benefited from an allocation in the previous year for building works.
    Action: the committee will review the grant request and present their recommendation in the June meeting.
3   Karen Anderson gave an update on the planned concert in the park to be held in July. She reported that volunteers were needed to distribute leaflets for the event and requested funding of $900 to pay for Folder Display Services for printing. Larry Wiedemann suggested contacting local colleges for distribution. Discussion ensued as to whether the volunteers were to be paid. It was agreed that volunteers would be given free tickets.
    Action: Karen to go ahead with the printing. Larry to contact student organizations and recruit volunteers.
4   Richard Keller announced that the new area website was now live and that the mobile apps for the iPhone and Android have been successfully launched. The mobile website has been revamped with a 'Find things nearby' function. Jerry Lucas felt that there was a need to provide information on restaurants on the VisitourRegion.com webpages and include a specialty/culinary experience section that would include things such as food festivals and local gastronomy. Jodi Ruzicka agreed in principle but pointed out that dining is more suitable for a navigational app on a smartphone, as consumers will be looking for a restaurant once they have arrived at their location or destination.
    Action: Richard Keller to look into this topic and contact restaurants to find out if they are willing to pay to be listed.
5   There being no other business, the meeting closed at 4.10 p.m. The next meeting will be held on 5 June at 2.00 p.m. in the administration building.

Describing a heritage site

A description of a historic monument or place of outstanding natural beauty can be organized in different ways. However, most heritage site descriptions contain the following information:

- a geographic description
- a number of significant dates
- the features of the site
- why the site is felt to be important

Stonehenge

Located in southwest England, Stonehenge is probably Europe's most famous prehistoric site. Built in several stages as from 5,000 years ago, it consists of four-metre high standing stones capped by huge horizontal blocks and arranged in a horseshoe pattern. A second circle of bluestones was added around 2,000–1,550BCE, having been transported from a site 240 kilometres away.

We can only guess at the significance of the site and the rituals that may have taken place but the alignment of the stones leaves little doubt that whoever built Stonehenge had precise astronomical knowledge of the path of the sun at midsummer sunrise and midwinter sunset. For this reason, Stonehenge may have had religious significance as a place of sun worship. Following a recent excavation, it is also thought that the site could have been erected as a temple with unique healing powers. There is evidence that people suffering from illness and disease came from great distances to the site, perhaps as pilgrims seeking a cure.

Stonehenge and the nearby stone circle at Avebury are listed as World Heritage sites not only for their sophisticated architectural construction but also because of evidence of a highly organized prehistoric society. Stonehenge's monumental scale is all the more impressive, given that the only tools available were made of wood, stone and bone. The labour involved in extracting, transporting and erecting the stones indicates that the builders must have been able to command immense resources and control large numbers of people during the long period of construction.

Legal documents

Most legal documents are drafted by lawyers but it is important to be aware of the kind of language used in contracts and what the legal terms mean. The text below is a travel agreement signed between a tour operator and a travel agency, giving the agency the right to sell a package holiday.

THIS TRAVEL AGREEMENT is entered into on (*effective date*)
BETWEEN: MediTours, a private limited company whose registered office is at (*place*)
AND: Urizen Travel, a division of the Ahania Group, whose registered office is at (*place*).

WHEREAS this Travel Agreement sets forth the relationship between the Parties and their respective rights, duties and obligations, it is hereby agreed as follows:

MediTours authorize Urizen Travel to organize a group tour to Turkey from (*date*) to (*date*) for a maximum of (*number*) people. The price of the said tour shall be fixed at €1,199 per passenger, in accordance with the provisional schedule (see Appendix 1) and subject to the terms and conditions hereunder.

In conformity with the legislation in force, Urizen Travel reserves the right to make all necessary modifications to the itinerary and to postpone or cancel the tour in exceptional circumstances beyond its control, such as but not limited to:
• strike, riot or civil commotion and any consequence of war in the countries concerned
• unforeseen adverse meteorological conditions affecting transport
• breaches of contract by air carriers or providers of local services.

Urizen Travel shall have the right, subject to prior justification, to modify the tour prices as a result of currency fluctuations, rising fuel prices and any and all unexpected increases in charges made by the suppliers of local services.

As a result of which, MediTours may, if deemed advisable, cancel the tour at no extra expense, should the said increase exceed 5% in total.

Payment shall be staggered as follows:
• 25% on signature of the present agreement
• 25% 3 months prior to departure
• 50% 35 days prior to the date of departure

Should Urizen Travel withdraw from the present agreement, any monies paid to MediTours shall remain the property of MediTours and cannot be reclaimed.

This Agreement shall be governed by and construed in accordance with English law and the Parties irrevocably accept and agree that any action based upon any claim of breach arising out of or in connection with this Agreement will be subject to and within the jurisdiction of the English courts.

---

used at the beginning of a contract to mean 'considering that'

explains in a clear, organized way (= sets out)

the people making the agreement. Capital letters are used for words that the writer considers important.

Words beginning with *here* + a preposition are frequent in contracts (e.g. *herein, hereafter, hereinafter, hereunder*).

previously mentioned

In legal documents, *shall* means *must*.

Lawyers make sure nothing is omitted by joining words with similar meanings (e.g. *any and all, null and void, power and authority*).

failure to comply with the terms and conditions

depending on

judged or considered to be

if

interpreted

without being able to change their mind

the legal authority to hear cases and make decisions

CVs

The following tips are useful when deciding how to lay out and format your CV according to the conventions of modern international business culture.

- Use headings to help you lay out the information in a clear and concise way.
- Use bullet points.
- Put the most recent information first.
- List the skills you've acquired.
- Use action verbs (e.g. *managed*, *monitored*, *planned*, *supervised*).
- Avoid abbreviations and jargon.
- Do not translate qualifications, places or institutions into English.
- Keep everything to one A4 page.
- Proofread your CV twice. Check for mistakes in grammar, spelling and punctuation.

CV

Rebecca Tyndale

✉ 29 Barker Street, Randwick, Sydney 2031
• 02 9382 4022
💻 r.tyndale@gtsmail.com
DOB 02/04/1987

Career goal
Tourism professional, experienced in Strategic Event and Tourism Management, seeks challenging international position in hospitality. Willing to relocate at short notice.

Skills
- proven ability to work under pressure and meet deadlines
- conscientious and methodical, with a good eye for detail
- positive attitude, good team player, capable of working autonomously
- excellent spoken and written communication skills; fluent in French, German and Spanish

Work experience
2012–2013 Action World, Sydney
Reporting to the Event Director, I was responsible for:
- planning, recruiting and coordinating staff for VIP events.
- selecting locations and organizing international cultural exchange programmes.
- setting budgets, outsourcing supplies and monitoring costs.

2010–2011 Sylvan Parks, UK
Events coordinator in charge of:
- handling inventory and liaising with suppliers.
- training new employees in all aspects of customer care.
- supervising day-to-day operations and leisure activities.

Education and qualifications
2009–2010: MSc in Events, Tourism and Hospitality Management, Macquarie University
2006–2009: Diploma in Hospitality Management, Canberra School of Tourism

Interests
bodybuilding, sailing, water sports

Referees
available on request

Restaurant menus

When composing a restaurant menu, it is important to make the food sound as appetizing as possible while at the same time making it clear what the dishes contain so that diners are not surprised or disappointed.

Many restaurants use French terms to make the food sound more gastronomic, for example, *tenderloin of lamb avec sauce à la menthe*; the French term is an exact translation of 'with mint sauce' but it sounds more exotic. Menus may use the French term *concassé* to describe chopped vegetables or *coulis* to describe a pressed mixture of vegetables or fruit.

It is always a good idea to describe food items in language that is easy to understand but vivid and appetizing. Use adjectives such as *tender, juicy, rich, satisfying*, etc. to give a flavour to the descriptions but be careful not to overuse them. You can employ additional appetizing vocabulary when you discuss menu choices with diners.

Break the menu into sections. These could be *Starters*, *Main courses* and *Desserts* or, if the restaurant offers a wide variety of foods, you may need main sections (*Breakfast, Lunch, Dinner*) and subsections (*Fish, Poultry, Vegetarian, Pasta* and *Salads*). Use adjectives to give a flavour to the descriptions.

GASTRONOMIC MENU

──○ Starters ○──

MEAT

Slices of roast beef served with garlic mayonnaise and a beetroot salad

Salad of smoked duck breast and foie gras with baby beetroots,
pickled turnips and apple purée

FISH AND SEAFOOD

Fresh crab meat, topped with turnip leaves in a sweet and sour sauce

Caramelized scallops on a bed of mashed violet potatoes,
served with a thick pumpkin cream

──○ Main courses ○──

Sirloin steak, grilled and peppered, served with glazed woodland mushrooms,
ripe cherry tomatoes, fresh watercress and hand-cut French fries

Chicken pan-fried in extra-virgin olive oil and simmered in a ground black
pepper sauce; served with a mixed salad and appetizing crusty garlic bread

Spanish-style grilled cheese with smoky paprika roasted pepper
and delicious tomato topping

Asparagus and scampi risotto: a creamy rice dish with large freshly-caught
shrimps, served with sautéed onions and carrots

──○ Desserts ○──

Vanilla crème brûlée with spring raspberries and tangy lemon ice cream

Luxury rhubarb crumble, served with piping hot custard

Caramelized apples on a puff pastry base, served with whipped cream

Home-made chocolate cake with a strawberry coulis

Lemon cheesecake topped with shortbread cookie crumbs
and dusted with powdered sugar

PAIRWORK FILES

File 1, unit 1, page 13

STUDENT A

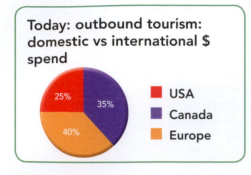

Today: outbound tourism: domestic vs international $ spend

- USA — 25%
- Canada — 35%
- Europe — 40%

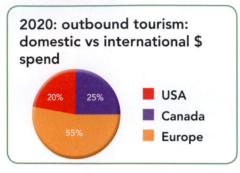

2020: outbound tourism: domestic vs international $ spend

- USA — 20%
- Canada — 25%
- Europe — 55%

File 2, unit 2, page 17

STUDENT A

Features of a well-designed website

- It should be possible for the site to be displayed on different web browsers and on different devices. Make sure it can be viewed on a smartphone.
- If real-time data is important, the site should be linked to a database for automatic updates.
- Visitors skim-read online. Use lots of subtitles and bulleted lists. Do not display more than about 250 words of text on a page and make sure there are no spelling mistakes.
- Make personal information and order forms easy to find and fill in.
- Do not display visitor number counters on your site. It is amateurish.
- Have access to you own site. Make sure you can update it yourself rather than using external specialists or you will be charged every time you want to make any changes.

File 3, unit 2, page 18

STUDENT B

1 'People are being bombarded by messages. Most are put in the trash as soon as they are received.'

2 'The use of social media is just a fad; it will soon be replaced by something else, just like MP3s replaced CDs, which replaced vinyl records, which replaced ...'

3 'Social media are primarily "social" and interpersonal, not an unsolicited commercial marketing channel.'

4 'It's impossible to translate the number of tweets and shares into tangible sales.'

5 'A great deal of time is needed to monitor a social media campaign; and time is money.'

6 'How do you know that that great hotel or restaurant review wasn't written by the owner?'

7 'Social networks are no good for direct selling or marketing. Customers are turned off by the hard sell.'

File 4, unit 4, page 33

STUDENT A

Sustainable tourism proposals

- Waste disposal: provide litter bins in villages and along beaches. Create a recycling plant (five tons a day: 57 percent reused).
- Water treatment: create a facility so all water used by hotels, etc. is reused for irrigation.
- Building: enforce a ban on all building along the coast within 300 metres of the high tide line
- Hotels: stop the licensing of any new luxury hotels and resorts in the area. Provide incentives for Goans to set up small guesthouses.
- Second homes: limit the construction of holiday homes and impose a tax on existing properties.
- Tourism watch: set up a committee to monitor the impacts of tourism and mobilize the community when their interests are threatened.
- Homestay holidays: provide the opportunity for tourists to live with a local family, experience Goan life and learn traditional music, crafts and cooking.

File 5, unit 4, page 39

STUDENT B

You are the mayor of Mali Brijun. You see advantages and disadvantages.

Advantages

* employment: 75 jobs created during the two years of construction
* finance: public money from the Croatian Tourist Board – no increase in local taxes but an ecotax can be levied on tourists
* politics: can 'steal' tourists from the mayor of Veliki Brijun

Disadvantages

* few permanent jobs, if any; not all jobs may be for local people
* investment could be used for a conference centre (more profitable)
* profits from dinosaur park would go to private investors, not the local community
* wind power is not very ecological, and some say noisy and ugly

File 6, unit 5, page 45

STUDENT A

1 You are an angry passenger and are talking to Student B, a supervisor employed by the airline.

* You have missed your flight to Cracow because the scheduled airport shuttle bus from your hotel did not turn up.
* You took the next bus but arrived 15 minutes after check-in had closed and the clerk refused to put you on the flight. She also refused to speak to the captain.
* You want to be put on the next available flight and bumped up to first class in compensation.
* You paid £15 for the bus ride and are demanding reimbursement. You maintain that the bus company acts as an agent for the airline.

2 You are a supervisor employed by the airline and are talking to Student B, an angry passenger.

* You have no control of the staff at the other airport and regret the passenger was treated badly.
* The airline will refund the cost of the flight and possibly offer compensation.
* You have some forms the passenger can fill in to claim on the insurance.
* The bus is due in about an hour. You will call a minicab company if there are not enough seats for everyone.

File 7, unit 7, page 65

STUDENT B

You and Student C are events coordinators with Apotheosis. This is your detailed price list. Explain to Student A, Smartset's CEO, what each item involves and advise him/her accordingly.

Venue	
Oakland Manor	$10,000 (7 p.m.–12 a.m.)
Rockridge Conference Centre	$7,500 (6 p.m.–10 p.m.)

Entertainment	
Music	
Classical string quartet	$1,800
Local rock band	$950
DJ and Emcee	$275/hour
Cabaret	
Belly dancers	$50/hour
Fire eaters	$40/hour
Stand-up comedian	$35/hour

File 8, unit 7, page 67

STUDENT A

You are Nick. You have decided to enlist the help of Global Productions, an events management company. You send the email below. Read it and list the points on which you need advice. Write a suggested agenda for your meeting with Global Productions.

Basically, I need advice on how to make the festival break even. There's the threat of legal action hanging over me and a number of bands have deserted the cause. We get good attendances but maybe I need to think more about promotion, a new sponsor, ticketing and so on.

There's also the problem of safety and making sure that the festival runs smoothly in terms of the sale of food and drink, policing, personnel, crowd control and so on. I've always relied on volunteer staff but it's difficult to coordinate so many people and I sometimes don't even know where they are!

But the biggest headache is the choice of venue as it still hasn't been decided and I'd be grateful for any suggestions.

Looking forward to our meeting next week.

File 9, unit 5, page 47

GROUP B

From:	Judith Coleman, Operations
To:	Nigel Foreman
Subject:	Working party meeting

I understand you discussed the issue of check-in kiosks and security issues. At present, all passengers travelling domestically, together with checked and carried-on baggage, are screened for weapons, explosives and other prohibited items. This is more effective than identity checking at deterring and preventing security incidents. The issue raised by the report is about policing and alleged criminal activity, not about airport security.

A ban on e-ticketing and a return to identity checks would cause further delays as most domestic carriers have moved towards internet check-in and dedicated self-check-in kiosks. We should go ahead and install these kiosks asap.

Airports have large fixed infrastructure costs, and studies have demonstrated that unit costs decline significantly as traffic increases up to 1.5 million Work Load Units (WLU, defined as a passenger or 100 kg of freight) per annum. Consequently, the greater the number of passengers and goods passing through the airport, the greater the profit.

Airport expansion could create 500 jobs

According to the RAA, the proposed extension of Claybourne Airport will provide job opportunities for some 500 in the county, ranging from ground handling crews, aircraft maintenance and security personnel to check-in and retail sales staff. Observers greeted the news enthusiastically given the chronic 17 percent unemployment rate across the region.

Key industry facts

Non-aeronautical revenue is growing much faster than aeronautical income or traffic figures and producing greater profit margins. Additional income from non-aeronautical sources is a key component in enabling airports to generate funds for the investment they must undertake in terminal and airfield expansion. The commercial revenue stream is essential for positive credit ratings and the airport's ability to attract finance for large infrastructure projects.

Case of Plane Absurd v. Beaconsfield Airport

European court of human rights
(Application no. 36022/97)
Article 86
The Chamber held that, whatever analytical approach was adopted, regard must be had to the fair balance that had to be struck between the competing interests of the individual and the community as a whole. Further, in the particularly sensitive field of environmental protection, mere reference to the economic wellbeing of the country was not sufficient to outweigh the rights of others. The Chamber considered that States were required to minimize, as far as possible, interference with Article 8 rights, by trying to find alternative solutions and by generally seeking to achieve their aims in the least onerous way as regards human rights.

From:	CEO
To:	Human resources

The capital investment in the planned expansion means that payroll costs must be kept to an absolute minimum and any employee leaving must not be replaced.

File 10, unit 7, page 63

STUDENT A

You are the CEO of Smartset. You would like to:
- invite all the staff (but maybe not their partners?).
- learn about a suitable venue.
- provide some form of entertainment, possibly a cabaret.
- find out about equipment and seating arrangements.
- have a sit-down dinner for staff and guests.
- discuss how many staff will be needed.
- decide on a suitable date.

The aim of the discussion is to have an overall view of what can be provided. Detailed discussions will follow in a later meeting.

File 11, unit 4, page 33

STUDENT B

Sustainable tourism proposals

- Water use: ban the construction of hotel pools and golf courses (an 18-hole golf course uses enough water to cover the irrigation needs of 100 farmers!). Enforce a hosepipe ban in periods of drought.
- Music and dance: prohibit unauthorized moonlight rave parties. In order to promote the region's cultural heritage, create a 'World Music Festival', incorporating a fusion of Western and Eastern music and dance genres.
- Information centre: set up a location where tourists are briefed on the need to be responsible in their contacts with the host community and environment.
- Beach vendors: regulate and licence the use of stalls, bars and restaurants. Pull down unlicensed establishments.
- Solidarity tourism: offer alternative packages whereby tourists experience the real Goa. These tours would foster authentic cultural encounters with the community using local guides.
- Casinos: organize a protest against the plan to licence the operation of floating casinos along the coast.
- Transport: encourage hotels and operators to use local taxi drivers. Provide interest-free loans to disadvantaged youths to buy a rickshaw and create their own business.

File 12, unit 4, page 39

STUDENT C

You are a member of the Croatian Wildlife Association. In your opinion, the proposed eco-resort would spoil the environment. In particular, you are against:

- the destruction of 20 hectares of forest (some species of plants are close to extinction and many trees are very old).
- the construction of a road as no vehicles can at present access the site.
- any modern facilities. You feel that ecotourism should be 'back to nature'.
- any boating (especially the use of motorboats) in the area as it disturbs the marine life.
- cycling on the island as this destroys or frightens wildlife.

You would support the construction of basic lodges or cabins for bird-watching and similar activities.

File 13, unit 8, page 69

STUDENT B

On-TrackTours, an award-winning travel provider for the young seniors market, is seeking an **investigations executive** to be in charge of handling customer complaints, researching issues with suppliers, requesting appropriate compensation and maintaining detailed records.

Your duties will involve:
- dealing with customer grievances.
- liaising with internal departments to resolve supplier issues.
- forwarding the complaint to the supplier/hotelier responsible and requesting compensation.
- chasing the response by email and telephone.

Interested? The person we require must be well-educated and computer-literate. A previous track record in the travel industry is beneficial but more important are your strong communication skills, methodical approach, integrity and ability to multitask while working under pressure.

Salary negotiable, depending on age and experience. Fringe benefits include subsidized staff restaurant and a childcare subsidy.

File 14, unit 7, page 65

STUDENT C

You and Student B are events coordinators with Apotheosis. This is your detailed price list. Explain to Student A, Smartset's CEO, what each item involves and advise him/her accordingly.

Equipment and fixtures

Sound system and lighting	$2,000
Trestle tables (seats:10 cm)	$8 each
Floral décor for tables	$30 each

Catering

Traditional roast beef dinner	$32.50/person
Finger buffet (self-service)	$22.75/person
Vegetarian meal	$19.50/person

Personnel

Security staff	$20/hour each
Serving/Reception staff	$15/hour each

Payment

half of fee due on signature of contract; the rest seven days after the event

File 15, unit 8, page 75

STUDENT B

Name: Graham Nash
Age: 33
Nationality: American
Marital status: married; one child, wife pregnant
Education: Obtained a scholarship to do a Bachelor's degree at the Chaplin School of  Hospitality and Tourism, Florida. Obtained GPA of 3.7 and cum laude.
Experience: Did a number of internships in spa resorts and hotels close to the Walt Disney World theme park, Orlando. Worked for three years as a customer services manager for an American domestic airline. Has been working recently as a freelance tour guide in London. He says he knows he is overqualified for his present job but came to Europe to gain experience.
Languages: native English, fluent spoken and written Spanish, some French
Salary expectations: 15 percent more than average
Interests: Photography, vegetarian cuisine. Has been on a residential yoga teacher training course at the Samahita Retreat.
Interview notes: Ambitious, versatile, passionate about future directions in the wellness industry. Said at the interview that he needs to earn a lot more to support his family and is looking for a job that has management potential. His ambition is to open up his own spa and meditation centre in Nepal.

Name: Carmen Rosa
Age: 35
Nationality: Mexican
Marital status: divorced, living with a new partner; no children
Education: Higher Vocational Qualification in Hospitality Management and Tourism from the EIDE in Santurtzi, northern Spain
Experience: Was married to the owner of the El Pueblito Spa Resort in Samaipata, Bolivia and worked with him for ten years in a number of capacities (receptionist, accountant, front and back office). Since she arrived in this country, she has done a number of unrelated temporary jobs. At present unemployed and finishing a course in thalassotherapy.
Languages: Native Spanish. Passed the University of Cambridge ESOL Certificate in Advanced English (grade B).
Salary expectations: willing to work for what we offer
Interests: beauty treatments, historical novels, DIY
Interview notes: Initially reserved but intelligent, motivated and ambitious. Interviewed well and is obviously experienced in dealing with both people and finance. Largely self-taught and capable of working autonomously. I had the impression that she would be hard-working, reliable and perfectionist.

File 16, unit 8, page 75

I was Ms Watson's employer at OzTours in Sydney. During her time with us, she was conscientious and methodical but showed little initiative. She has an outgoing personality and the nature of the work was perhaps not suited to her temperament. She is vivacious, with a friendly, outgoing personality but needs to be stimulated.

Carmen was employed for six months in our office last year. Despite going through a traumatic divorce, she was a real asset to our organization. She has excellent written and verbal communication skills, is extremely organized and can work independently. Carmen effectively scheduled and supervised several office assistants, who were responsible for many of the office's basic administrative and clerical functions, and she ensured that the work was carried out efficiently.

It is my pleasure to recommend Graham Nash for employment with your organization. I was Graham's supervisor for over two years, during which time he worked as a customer services manager. I have been consistently impressed with his ability to multitask and deal calmly and efficiently with harassed passengers. I wish him every success in his desire to promote the virtues of Ayurvedic medicine for wellness and a healthy work–life balance.

I have known Carlos de Sousa in a variety of capacities over the years. He is extremely competent and has an excellent rapport with people of all ages. I have no doubt that his extensive experience would be enormously beneficial to your hotel.

File 17, unit 9, page 81

STUDENT A

You are the manager of the East Quay restaurant. You have read the review below on a social networking site. Conduct a feedback session with the server, Student B.

We had a meal on 12 July at the East Quay restaurant down by the river. There were about 15 diners at different tables and just one server.

My husband ordered a soda and I asked for an iced tea with lemon. The server quickly came back with our drinks but not my lemon. Then I asked for the shrimp to start and the fish dinner with fries, and my husband had the T-bone steak. We had to wait about 25 minutes and I could hear her telling the cook to hurry up. Then she came back and started a conversation with other diners about a night out in the local disco. Finally, she came back to our table but we did not get our shrimp starter. I asked where it was and she said, 'I don't know.' She went back and yelled at the cook. When she returned, she said, 'I guess the cook forgot it, and I don't know where he is. We are so busy.' When she asked, 'Do you still want them?' my response was 'No!'

Also, when our food came, the fries came with mayonnaise on them. Nowhere in the menu does it say that the fries come with mayonnaise and I am allergic to egg-based products. So, I asked her nicely to get some fries without it. She rolled her eyes and said, 'OK.' Needless to say, she did not get a tip and looked at me rudely when we left.

File 18, unit 9, page 83

STUDENT B

This probably goes without saying but do not drink the water out of the tap! This is especially difficult when you're brushing your teeth – old habits die hard. But you'll regret it if you forget, as I did at our hotel and suffered the consequences! Maybe you should warn people before they leave.

I felt terrible in Cuzco – couldn't breathe properly and had a severe headache. Luckily, a pharmacy prescribed Diamox and I felt better. Cuzco is above 3,000 m in elevation, so it's easy to suffer from dehydration. Maybe you should tell visitors to drink coca herbal tea and chew coca leaves to alleviate some of the problems with high altitude sickness.

I enjoyed the tour and the food was fabulous but why waste time travelling to Machu Picchu when you can get there from Cuzco by helicopter? It only takes 45 minutes!

I enjoyed the tour but it was all too brief. Just one cookery class didn't really give us the opportunity to learn more than a couple of dishes. The time spent in the sacred valley was far too short to properly appreciate the site and just one day at the Mistural festival was insufficient.

Why not propose a basic tour but offer optional add-ons? I imagine that all visitors to Peru want to visit Machu Picchu but for foodies, the high point is surely the cookery classes, the culinary activities and the Mistural. Why not just stay in Lima for the basic gastronomic experience and do the other things at the end of the stay for people who want to do the Inca trail?

File 19, unit 10, page 89

STUDENT A

Read the information about the situation at the hotel and prepare for your interview with Student B, the journalist, to talk about the crisis. Remember to follow the guidelines for talking to the media in Exercise 4.

- After two days of torrential rain, the hotel was inundated at 7.45 a.m. today by floodwaters bursting through the lobby and rising up to the first floor.

- Snakes were seen swimming up the stairwell and one woman was bitten on the leg. She has been taken to hospital and is not in any danger.

- You have evacuated the remaining guests and are providing them with alternative accommodation.

- The guests on the ground and first floor have lost their passports and most of their belongings have been damaged. Consular and crisis staff are providing assistance.

- The names of all the guests affected have been communicated to their next of kin. They are being kept informed of developments via text messages and updates on your website.

- The guests weren't evacuated beforehand because it is now February and the cyclone season normally runs from May to November. Tropical cyclones can occur outside this period but this area has never been affected.

- You have always been committed to providing maximum security for guests and regularly meet hotel staff to discuss emergency procedures.

File 20, unit 1, page 13

STUDENT B

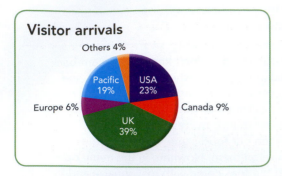

Visitor arrivals

File 21, unit 2, page 17

STUDENT B

Features of a well-designed website

- Uniform design: a good website is clear and easy to navigate. Each page looks as if it belongs to the same site.
- Easy navigation: visitors should not have to hunt for information. Include an index, menu bar or set of navigation buttons on your home page. Do not underline text so that it looks like a link.
- Colours, fonts and alignment: too many colours and font sizes are distracting, which can result in the visitor leaving the site. All text should be left-aligned.
- Contact information: contact information should be easy to find and on every page. Give visitors different ways to reach you. Publish your full postal address. This reassures visitors that you really exist.
- Images and video: a good website is not cluttered with graphics and photos. The visitor should immediately have a sense of what the information is and where to find it. If a visitor has to wait too long for images or video to load, he or she will leave. Some devices do not have Flash Player and avoid plug-ins at all costs.
- Not too many bells and whistles: animated graphics, pop-up windows and the like may be fun but they can look unprofessional. How many times have you clicked on 'Skip intro' or a video clip that got stuck?

File 22, unit 5, page 45

STUDENT B

1 You are a supervisor employed by the airline and are talking to Student A, an angry passenger.

- You cannot believe that the shuttle bus was late. It is always on time and no passengers, to your knowledge, missed the plane because of a late bus.
- You have made enquiries. The clerk did not refuse to speak to the captain. The aircraft was parked far from the departure lounge and a bus had taken the passengers to the plane waiting on the tarmac.
- You may be able to upgrade the passenger to first class if there are any available seats.
- The bus company is independently run and the passenger should take up the matter of compensation with them.

2 You are an angry passenger and are talking to Student A, a supervisor employed by the airline.

- You have arrived from Amsterdam having already experienced a seven-hour delay. At the airport you were given a voucher which allowed you to purchase just one sandwich and a soft drink.
- You were offloaded from one plane because the airline didn't have a big enough jet to accommodate all the passengers from two other flights that had been cancelled. Your bag was thrown onto the tarmac in the pouring rain. When you complained, the ground staff told you to keep your mouth shut and get on the plane.
- Now your connecting domestic flight has been cancelled because the plane is being used on another route. It seems you will have to travel by bus.
- Judging by the number of passengers stranded like yourself at the airport, you don't understand how you will all be able to get on one bus. And what about your luggage?

File 23, unit 6, page 59

STUDENT B

Inventory
- a plan of Ascoby Hall in 1432
- a number of stuffed animals
- remains of Roman clay pottery and mosaics
- Saxon axe heads, helmets and shields
- an 18th-century inkpot and writing materials
- audio recordings of local residents (mid 20th century)
- a book on the origin of place names
- a collection of Viking and Saxon coins and medals
- a skeleton of a Roman soldier, with sword and helmet
- copies of letters written by members of the Gentlemen's Society
- prints and paintings showing life during the 15th century
- a list of words that used to be spoken in the local dialect

File 24, unit 7, page 63

STUDENT B

You are an events coordinator with Apotheosis. You can provide:

- a choice of venues: Oakland Manor (a beautiful listed building with gardens; capacity: 900) or Rockridge Conference Centre (modern building; capacity: 1,000).
- a choice of music: classical music, a rock group, a DJ and disco.
- the hire of equipment (sound systems and lighting, tables and chairs, etc.).
- cabaret artists (belly dancers, fire eaters, stand-up comedians).
- catering: a choice of meals (banquet-style or finger buffet). Detailed menus available.
- security, reception and catering staff (a ratio of 1 : 30 guests).

You have a price list for each service but the first thing is to discuss what type of event would be most suitable for the employees. The detailed costing comes at a later stage.

File 25, unit 8, page 69

STUDENT C

Howatt Hotels is a fast-expanding international hotel group with 42 properties in Europe and on the Asian continent. We are now looking for an ambitious, high-flying **operations manager** to join our senior management team in Dubai. He or she will play a key role in contributing to the profitability of the hotel through the monitoring of revenue and budgets, maintaining effective cost controls and creating an environment where the staff are motivated to maximize sales.

Responsibilities include:
- identifying and following up all sales leads.
- keeping the team up-to-date concerning hotel and company activities through daily communications, including financial and customer feedback.
- conducting interviews and contributing to recruitment decisions.

The person appointed must have a solid background in the hotel industry, be standards-driven and detail-oriented, with the ability to organize in a logical manner and plan ahead. He or she is hard-working, articulate, has first-rate leadership and people-management skills, and is focused on providing a consistently high standard of customer service.

An excellent remuneration package is available, including profit-related bonuses, company car and private medical insurance.

File 26, unit 7, page 67

STUDENT B

You are a representative of Global Productions, an events management company. You have made some investigations and can make some proposals to Nick Ikin.

Venue
Selangor racecourse: 30–45 minutes from Kuala Lumpur depending on traffic; good parking at the racecourse – buses and taxis also available; easy crowd control, good signage, toilet facilities; hire for weekend: AUD 100,000

Ticketing
ticket-only entry; tickets available over the internet and record stores; AUD 40 each

Promotion
dedicated website and radio stations (e.g. last.fm); advertising in local and international music magazines (need to write a press release)

Catering
allow only licensed traders; charge fee for their presence on the site; ensure supply of water and electricity

Estimated visitor numbers
based on previous estimates: 15,000

Personnel
volunteers need to be clear as to their role and equipped with smartphones/walkie-talkies; employ an agency to clean up site; recruit security staff from an agency and professionals for stage set-up

Line-up
all bands to be given proper contracts with penalty clauses if they withdraw without valid reason; limit number to 15; pay standard fee of AUD 25,000, with 20 percent extra for two top names

Finance
Warped Vinyl Records interested in promoting Asian music and have agreed to gift ten percent of receipts from MP3 downloads of bands performing at the festival who sign up to their label; sponsorship needed from local firms likely to be viewed favourably by target audience; allow advertising on tickets, programmes, stands, stages, etc.

Objectives
profit through ticketing, sponsorship, space rental, etc.; encouraging tourism; building up reputation of festival over time through an annual event

File 27, unit 9, page 81

STUDENT B

You are a server at the East Quay restaurant. Your manager, Student A, wants to talk to you about an incident with a couple of diners on the evening of 12 July.

- You were on your own that evening as the other waiting staff were absent. There were about 20 diners and you were rushed off your feet.

- A couple ordered shrimp starters, which the cook took a long time to do. You did your best to get the order to the table quickly by talking to the cook and explained why it was taking so long.

- You think the cook needs an assistant to help with the starters and desserts.

- In the end the couple said they didn't want the starters because they took a long time to prepare but then the woman made a fuss about mayonnaise with her fries in her main course. You don't think it's possible to be allergic to mayonnaise and no one has ever complained about serving mayonnaise on the side before. The woman was making a fuss about nothing as the mayonnaise was not actually on the fries. You felt she was aggressive but agreed to replace the fries, this time without mayonnaise.

File 28, unit 10, page 89

STUDENT B

You are a journalist. There have been reports of a flood in a hotel affecting package holiday tourists and you have the opportunity to interview Student A, the local representative of the tour operator. Prepare your questions for the interview. You would like to know:

- when exactly the flooding started and what the consequences have been.

- how the situation has evolved.

- what is being done to inform the guests' families.

- why the guests weren't evacuated beforehand.

- if flooding in this area is common.

- to what extent the hotel was prepared for this kind of incident.

GRAMMAR REFERENCE

Continuous aspect

1 The continuous (or progressive) aspect deals with time in progress at the moment of speaking and perceives actions and events as incomplete, temporary or developing. It is expressed by the appropriate form of *be + verb + -ing*.

2 Use the continuous aspect to talk about:

an action in progress at the moment of speaking.

*Can you call back later? I'm **having** lunch.*

trends and situations that are changing.

*The number of people doing adventure tourism **is growing**.*

*The polar ice caps **have been melting** much faster than scientists **have been predicting**.*

future arrangements.

*I'm **meeting** their Chief Executive next Monday.*

temporary situations.

*Zhu's off sick so Pablo's **replacing** him until he gets better.*

*I've **been walking** to work while my car **is being** repaired.*

past situations that had not come to an end.

*During the 1960s people **were travelling** in increasing numbers.*

to describe past events repeated over time.

*Guests **were always complaining** about the noise, so we don't have a disco now.*

3 You can use continuous forms with modal verbs or the passive.

*The bus **should be arriving** shortly.*

*We **may be witnessing** a change in consumer preferences.*

*I'll **be using** public transport while my car **is being repaired**.*

4 Do not use the *-ing* form with stative verbs (verbs that describe a situation in which no obvious action takes place) such as *agree, believe, belong, depend, know, prefer, understand, want*. However, it is possible to use some stative verbs in the continuous form, when they have an active meaning or emphasize an ongoing situation. Compare:

*She **loves** her work and **thinks** it's useful.*

*She says she's **loving** her holiday and is **thinking** of staying an extra week. (Her holiday is not over and she hasn't decided yet.)*

Countable and uncountable nouns

Nouns belong to two major families: countable nouns and uncountable nouns. Countable nouns refer to things, people and ideas that are perceived as 'one' or 'more than one'. Uncountable nouns refer to things that are treated as indivisible wholes and not as separate objects.

COUNTABLE NOUNS

1 Countable nouns include:

individual objects, places, professions.

*There's **a lake** nearby where you can hire **a boat**.*

*She's **a receptionist**.*

units of measurement (*a metre, a mile, a litre, a gallon*, etc.).

***A pound** weighs less than **a kilo**.*

2 Use countable nouns with *a/an* or in the plural.

***Hotels** situated near **an exhibition centre** are usually booked well in advance.*

3 Countable nouns follow words such as *many, these, those, several, few* and *a few*.

*We have **several rooms** vacant at the moment.*

*Very **few people** come here in the low season.*

UNCOUNTABLE NOUNS

1 Uncountable nouns include:

food and drink seen as a whole and not as individual units.

*The Italians are famous for their **pasta**.*

*I never have **milk** or **sugar** in my **tea**.*

substances or materials (*glass, gold, marble, plastic, wood*, etc.).

*Ancient Greek sculptures were almost entirely made of **marble** or **bronze**.*

abstract ideas (*employment, health, insurance, progress, safety*, etc.).

*The travel industry is a good source of **employment**.*

*The legislation on **health** and **safety** is very strict.*

verbal nouns describing activities (*fishing, rafting, sailing, shopping*, etc.).

*Tourist attractions in the region include **fishing**, **bird-watching** and **hiking** in the foothills.*

2 Uncountable nouns do not have a plural form and take the singular form of the verb.

*Travel **broadens** the mind.*

*Information **is** power.*

3 Uncountable nouns follow words like *much*, *a little* and *little*.

> We don't have **much time**.
>
> There is very **little snow** in winter and not **much rain** either.

4 You can make an uncountable noun singular or plural by using another word or expression.

accommodation: a place to live

advertising: an advertisement/a commercial

advice: a piece of advice

information: a piece of information

insurance: an insurance policy

money: a coin/a banknote/a sum

progress: a step forward

training: a training course

travel: an excursion/a journey/a trip/a voyage

work: a job/a task

Making predictions

1 Use modal verbs to say that a future situation is certain, probable or possible.

certain

> The 21st century **will see** many changes in the tourism industry.
>
> The flight **won't be** on time because there was a maintenance problem.

probable

> We **may well see** more hotels using social media to interact with guests.
>
> There are no delays this morning, so your train **should be** here soon.

possible

> I have a meeting at 11.45, so I **may be** late for lunch.
>
> The sea **might be** rough today, so passengers **could be** seasick.

2 Use *be going to* to make firm predictions based on evidence at the time of speaking.

> Look at those clouds! I think it**'s going to rain**.

3 You can use expressions like *be bound to*, *there's a good chance*, *in all probability* and *be (highly) unlikely* to express different degrees of certainty.

> If you go to London, you**'re bound to** see a black taxi. (= certain)
>
> **There's a good chance** I'll have finished the report by tomorrow morning. (= in all probability)
>
> It**'s highly unlikely** for there to be hot weather in the north of Scotland, even in summer. (= it's very improbable)

Reporting verbs

1 Use reporting verbs to show the attitude of the person who spoke the original words. They give more information than just using *said*.

> 'I'll speak to her.' → He **promised** to speak to her.
>
> 'I'll give you a hand if you like.' → He **offered** to give me a hand.

2 Different reporting verbs are followed by different structures. They can be followed by:

a *that* clause. You can omit *that* from the clause.

> He **confirmed** (**that**) Monica is leaving.
>
> She **said** (**that**) she's found a better job.

a *to*-infinitive.

> She **threatened to resign**.

object + *to*-infinitive.

> He **advised the guest to leave** her valuables in the safe.

an *-ing* form.

> She **admitted making** a mistake.

Some verbs can be used with more than one structure.

> He **promised to help** us.
>
> He **promised** (**that**) he would help us.
>
> She **denied making** a mistake.
>
> She **denied** (**that**) she had made a mistake.

3 Reporting questions

To report *yes/no* questions, use *asked/wanted to know* + *if/whether*.

> 'Are you going to the exhibition?' → She **asked** (**me**) **if/whether** I was going to the exhibition.
>
> 'Do you have the flight details?' → He **wanted to know if/whether** I had the flight details.

To report questions that begin with *which, what, where, why, when, how*, etc., use the subject before the verb.

> 'Which airline are you using?' → She asked me which airline **I was** using. (NOT *was I using*)
>
> 'How much do you wish to spend?' → He wanted to know how much **they wished** to spend. (NOT *how much did they wish*)

4 Tenses in reported speech

When you report what someone said, you use tenses that relate to the time when you make the report. This often involves a change of tense: the verb is 'back-shifted' one step into the past.

> 'I **don't want** to go.' → Ivan said he **didn't want to go**.
>
> 'I**'ve written** to the client.' → Marisa told me she**'d written** to the client.

However, it is often unnecessary to change the tense in the following situations:

when the time reference is the same for the original speaker and the person reporting.

'I'm leaving next Wednesday.' → Osman says/said *he's leaving next Wednesday.* (Next Wednesday is in the future at the time of reporting.)

when the statement is true for all time.

'Venice is a beautiful place for a honeymoon.' → He said that Venice is a beautiful place for a honeymoon.

when there is already one 'back-shifted' verb in the sentence.

'I worked for TUI after I left college.' → He told me he'd worked for TUI when he left college. (NOT *he had left*)

The modal verbs *could, would, should, ought to* and *might* do not change in reported speech.

'It would be nice if we could meet again soon.' → She said it would be nice if we could meet again soon.

The passive

1 Form

The object of an active verb becomes the subject of a passive construction.

Active: *Thomas Cook invented **the package tour**.* (*the package tour* = object)

Passive: ***The package tour** was invented by Thomas Cook.* (*the package tour* = subject)

2 Use

Use the passive when you do not want to focus on who did the action or it is not necessary to know.

*The tower **was demolished** in 1753.*

*The missing passport **has been found**.*

*She **has been promoted** to the post of marketing director.*

If you want to mention who performs the action, use *by*.

*The missing passport has been found **by one of the cleaners**.*

Also use the passive to describe a process or procedure.

*First of all, when a vacancy **has been identified**, a job specification **is created** and a job advertisement **is written** and **published**. Candidates **are invited** to submit their CVs and suitable applicants **are** then **short-listed** and **may be invited** for interview.*

In an active sentence, the subject initiates the action.

***The resort representative** met the group at the airport.*

In a passive sentence, the starting point is the person or thing that is affected by the action.

***The group** was met at the airport by the resort representative.*

When writing in a formal style (e.g. reports, minutes of meetings), you may choose an impersonal style: *it* + passive.

***It was agreed** that the original plan should be altered.*

***It was considered** to be an acceptable alternative.*

***It has been decided** to postpone the meeting.*

Talking about the past

1 *Used to*

Use *used to* to talk about repeated past actions and situations that are no longer true.

*India **used to be** a British colony.*

*We **used to send** a lot of faxes but nobody does now.*

*There **used to be** a railway going through the village but it closed down.*

To form questions and negative sentences, use the auxiliary *did*.

***Did** Angola **use to belong** to Portugal?*

*I **didn't use to like** working on a cruise ship but now I enjoy the lifestyle.*

When *used to* is followed by a tag question, use the auxiliary *did*.

*You **used to work** with Henry, **didn't you**?*

2 *Would*

Would also refers to habitual actions and events in the past. However, with *would* there is often a previously-mentioned time frame, often established by an occurrence of *used to*, a verb in the past tense or a time-adverbial expression.

*When the family lived here in the 19th century, they used to dine in this room every evening. And after they had finished eating, the men **would retire** to the billiards room and the women **would sit** and talk.*

It is not possible to use *would* to refer to states.

*The town hall **used to be** a theatre.* (NOT *would be*)

Use the past simple, not *used to* or *would* when you want to say how many times something happened or that something happened at a specific time.

*I **went** on three training courses last year.* (NOT *I used to go*)

3 *It is believed/considered/said/thought …*

You can use *it is believed/considered/said/thought* followed by a *that* clause to make speculative statements about the past. This is a common feature of guided tours when ancient monuments and rumoured events are described.

It is thought (**that**) *the king of France slept in this room.*

It is believed (**that**) *the bell tower was a later addition.*

It is said that *the princess fell in love with one of her servants.*

Hypothetical situations

1 Use the third conditional to talk about imaginary past situations. Use the past perfect in the *if* clause and *would/could/might* + *have* + past participle in the main clause.

*If she **had spoken** to me earlier, I **might have been** able to help.*

*If they **hadn't taken** out insurance, they **couldn't have got** their money back.*

*If the plane **had arrived** on time, she **wouldn't have missed** her connection.*

*What **would** you **have done** if you **had known** about the situation?*

Do not use *would* in the *if* clause.

*If she **had spoken** to me earlier …* (NOT *If she would have spoken …*)

We can change the order of the clauses in conditional sentences.

*I **might have been** able to help if she **had spoken** to me earlier.*

*She **wouldn't have missed** her connection if the plane **had arrived** on time.*

2 In formal contexts, you can omit *if* and use *had* + subject + past participle.

Had you known *about the situation, what would you have done?*

3 You can also use mixed conditionals to talk about present hypothetical situations.

*If my boss **hadn't given** me a bad reference, I **would have** a much better job now.*

*If our previous chief executive **had stayed** with us, our company **would be** market leader.*

4 When describing a hypothetical situation, you can sometimes replace a past perfect construction with *if it weren't for …*

If it weren't for *Sushila, I wouldn't have managed to get everything ready on time.* (=*If Sushila hadn't helped me …*)

It is also possible to use *but for …*

But for *Sushila, I wouldn't have managed to get everything ready on time.*

Dependent prepositions

There are many verbs, adjectives and nouns which are followed by specific prepositions and it can be difficult to choose the right one. The table below gives examples of some of the more common combinations.

	Verbs	**Adjectives**	**Nouns**
for	I **apologise for** being late. They say the region's economy is **heading for** disaster.	She's **responsible for** health and safety. Sydney is **famous for** its opera house.	What's the **reason for** the extra charge? We have a **reputation for** luxury holidays at affordable prices.
from	This spray should **protect** you **from** mosquitoes. We're **suffering from** the competition.	She was **absent from** work yesterday. Our services are **different from** those of our competitors.	It makes a **change from** the usual routine. It's a lovely, secluded beach with **protection from** the wind.
of	I don't **approve of** overbooking. What did she **accuse** you **of** doing?	This painting is **typical of** the artist's work. I wasn't **aware of** the new regulations.	The **idea of** working for an airline appeals to me. There's little **chance of** getting tickets now.
on	The outcome doesn't **depend on** me. We all **congratulated** her **on** her promotion.	She likes Italian cooking but she's not **keen on** French cuisine. Your pay is **dependent on** your work experience.	The recession has had no **effect on** our sales. What are your **views on** the future of tourism?

	Verbs	Adjectives	Nouns
in	The campaign **succeeded in** boosting bookings. Our company **specializes in** adventure tourism.	Are you **interested in** going on a guided tour? The candidate was **lacking in** experience.	There has been an **increase in** the number of Chinese visitors. There's been a great deal of **interest in** our campaign.
to	She didn't **respond to** my email. They **invited** all their friends **to** their party.	A four-star hotel is **superior to** a two-star one. A small group is **preferable to** a large one.	Hard work is the **key to** success. What was your **reaction to** the idea?
with	I don't **agree with** you. How are you **coping with** the extra workload?	Are you **satisfied with** your stay so far? I'm **pleased with** your work.	We're having **problems with** our supplier. Do you need any **help with** the preparations?

Relative clauses

There are two kinds of relative clauses: defining and non-defining.

1 Defining relative clauses

A defining relative clause makes it clear which person or thing we are talking about.

The person **who/that gave me my first job** was a genius. (identifies a specific person)

The pyramids **which/that were built until the Third Dynasty** were made of mud and brick, not stone. (identifies particular pyramids)

Use *who* or *that* to refer to people. Use *which* or *that* to refer to things. Use *whose* to refer back to people or things.

It was a meeting **whose purpose I failed to understand**. (= I failed to understand its purpose.)

2 Non-defining relative clauses

A non-defining relative clause has extra, non-essential information. In this type of clause, use *who*, *which* and *whose* but not *that*. The relative clause is separated from the main clause by commas.

Hanna, **who is our receptionist,** will show you around the building.

The Rosetta stone, **which was found in 1799,** enabled Champollion to decipher the hieroglyphs.

Leonardo da Vinci, **whose painting of the Mona Lisa is world-famous,** was a great Italian artist and sculptor.

You can use *which* to refer back to a whole clause.

I'm afraid we've missed our train, **which means we'll be late.**

Modal verbs

SPECULATING

1 You can use the modal verbs *may*, *might*, *could*, *should* and *must* to say what you suppose to be true about the past or the present. For example, someone asks, 'Where is Juliette?' You could answer:

She **may/might/could be** in the back office. (= It's possible.)

She **should be** in the back office (= It's reasonably certain.)

She **must be** in the back office. (= It's pretty sure.)

She **can't be** in the back office. She called me from home five minutes ago. (= It's impossible.)

2 To refer to the past, use modal verb + *have* + past participle. For example, someone says, 'I can't find Juliette anywhere.' You could respond:

She **may/might/could have gone** out. (= It's possible.)

She **must have gone** out. (= It's pretty sure.)

She **can't have gone** out. She was right here a minute ago. (= It's impossible.)

It is not possible to use *should* to speculate about the past. *Should* + *have* + past participle expresses criticism.

She **should have gone** out. (= It was wrong for her to stay inside.)

3 It is also possible to speculate about the outcome of past situation by using a third conditional.

If I had anticipated the market trend a year ago, I **could/would/might have made** a fortune.

AUDIO SCRIPT

Unit 1

1.1

I = Interviewer, P = Paul Henley

I Can I ask you a simple question, Mr Henley? What motivates people to choose to go on vacation?

P Actually, it's not such a simple question. But it's a very important question because understanding what motivates people to visit specific places and do specific things has major economic consequences. I think we can identify three main reasons why people travel for leisure. First of all, they want to recharge their batteries, just get away, chill out and then come back refreshed. So, for instance, this might be a short break to a capital city like Rome. Second, they may be fulfilling a dream. For example, a couple has been saving up for a long time in order to go on a round-the-world cruise. We could call this 'wish fulfilment'. And thirdly, I think people often travel to gain prestige so that when they come back, they can impress their colleagues, friends or family. So, if they've been to some exotic destination like Easter Island or the Antarctic, they have something to talk about, to wow people with.

I OK, but maybe there are more noble reasons, like getting to know people who live in another country or learn about a different culture.

P Yes, but I'm afraid most tourists don't actually socialize with the local population, except very superficially. In fact, they probably spend most of their time on the beach or shopping.

1.2

I = Interviewer, P = Paul Henley

I I've heard of push factors and pull factors. Can you explain what these mean?

P Sure, the push factor is what makes you want to leave home, why you travel. It could include things like better weather, for British people; or a desire for adventure and to experience an activity that can't be found at home, like a safari, or for love and romance, like a honeymoon or a wedding abroad.

I And what about pull factors?

P These are the reasons why you choose a particular destination. It may be because the destination is relatively easy to get to, in terms of transport and time, or maybe the cost of living is attractive and you get more for your money than you would at home. Or maybe because the place is attractive in itself or is putting on a special event like the Olympics or the World Cup.

1.3

I = Interviewer, M = Monica Cheung

I So, are there any trends that have been emerging over the last ten years or so?

M Well, yes. Like everything else, the tourism industry is evolving in many different ways. One of the most important is the way that the internet has changed the way people organize and book their vacations: a lot of it is now personalized and done online. The High Street retail travel agent hasn't disappeared yet but is disappearing. Many travel agencies have gone out of business since the advent of internet bookings.

I Yes, that's true. What other trends have you identified?

M There's definitely been a growing trend towards more sustainable tourism, in particular, adventure tourism in countries where there hasn't yet been a significant tourism industry. So, governments in a lot of emerging countries are trying to attract foreign direct investment – countries like Bhutan, Nicaragua, the Dominican Republic or Sri Lanka. As a result, remote areas are being opened up, jobs are being created and revenues are being generated. The current trend towards adventure tourism and extreme sports in particular is expanding rapidly. It attracts young entrepreneurs and responds to a growing consumer demand.

I What about people? Have you seen any changes in the profile of tourists and their motivations?

M Yes, there's the tourist's demographic profile – the number of people over 55 has been increasing steadily in Europe, so the number of packages targeting senior citizens has been rising. I also think there's another important underlying trend: people are living under increased levels of stress, so they've been looking for activities to reduce the level of stress in their lives. So, we've seen a shift from recreational tourism products to more spiritual experiences like yoga or wellness vacations; people are increasingly looking for a meaning to their lives.

I What about the future?

M Well, a few years ago people were saying that the future lay in space travel, with people going to the moon or Mars, but I don't think any tourists will be staying on the moon in the foreseeable future. One major trend I think will be the gradual end of low-cost flights because of rising fuel prices. With the increased cost of flying, travel will develop parallels with the slow-food movement. We'll see more and more an appreciation of 'slow travel', with journeys by train, boat and bicycle gaining in popularity. People will be more interested in the journey itself rather than the restless striving for the next destination. As the poet TS Eliot once said, 'The journey, not the arrival, matters'.

1.4

Visuals are particularly useful when you are talking about statistics. You can use them to illustrate a relationship or make a comparison between things, while they are a powerful way to highlight a trend. So when you're giving a presentation, you need to display the visual and then comment on it so that everyone knows why you've displayed it.

There are a number of simple verbs you can use to introduce the topic. For example, *represent*, as in 'This bar chart represents the number of tourist arrivals in the world's most visited countries.' Or *show*, as in 'The pie chart shows visitor arrivals for the period in question.' Or you might use *portray*; for example, 'The red shaded segment portrays the number of visitors from New Zealand during the first semester.' Another useful verb is *illustrate*, as in 'The line graph illustrates the percentage change in profits over the last few years.' Another useful word is *breakdown*, meaning 'a list of all the separate parts of something', as in 'The table gives us a breakdown of residents entering Canada by land, air and sea.' All these are useful ways of referring to the image you're talking about.

1.5

H = Hannah, E = Expert, D = Dan

H As I explained on the phone, we're looking for some professional advice on how to attract Chinese tourists. So, could you tell us something about the profile of a typical outbound Chinese tourist and what their motivations are?

E Well, for the first ten years, when China opened up, tourists were mostly people travelling abroad for the very first time. They were the Generation X, people born, let's say, between 1960 and 1980. And the main question for the operator was how to put a package together at a price people could afford and that meant basically rock-bottom prices. For Generation X travellers, the opportunity to travel abroad was a status symbol, a once-in-a-lifetime thing and there wasn't much concern for quality because of the price factor. Well, there is still that market – basically, older people who want to visit as many countries as possible in ten days and are happy to stay in budget hotels. But I think we're now entering a second phase: there's a new profile of people who have a lot of money, are very active, go to expensive restaurants and so on – what we call Generation Y.

H In what other ways are they different from Generation X?

E Generation Y are in their mid-20s and they're the highly-educated 'connected' generation that's always been dominated by technology: they spend a lot of time on the internet and they've already abandoned the computer for the smartphone. They've probably already been to Europe a couple of times, maybe on business trips. So they want to do something more independent, more tailor-made to coincide with their leisure interests.

D OK, so whereabouts in China do these types of tourists come from? Can we make any generalizations?

E Actually, there's been a change in the pattern. In the past, 80 percent of Chinese wealth was in Shanghai and Beijing, and the other 20 percent in secondary cities with a population of less than ten million. So, most outbound Generation X tourists came from those two major cities. But now it's the opposite: 20 percent of the wealth is in Shanghai and Beijing and 80 percent in other places.

D That's important to know. So, how could you define the profile of this 80 percent?

E Well, they're the newly-rich. Unlike the older generation, who just wanted to go to the most famous places and see the typical sights, the younger generation is interested in showing that they've got money. They want to stay in luxury hotels with big lobbies and buy luxury branded goods and so on. They speak English and now they want more specialized products, a more authentic experience – they don't just want to follow the tour leader's flag.

H What kind of authentic experience do you have in mind?

E There's a whole new market for special interest groups, niche tourism – adventure vacations, golf vacations, nature tours, sports, ecotourism, things like that.

H OK, thanks, that's good to know.

1.6

K = Kevin, D = Dan, H = Hannah

K OK. So, we've now got quite a lot of information about travel motivations, accommodation preferences and so on. Is there anything else you've been able to find out? Dan?

D Yes. As we know, most Chinese visitors generally stay in relatively cheap hotels and the catering is not important. They really don't like the kind of food we eat – they may try European dishes once and then just avoid them. They often eat out together in a good local Chinese restaurant.

H Shopping is very important. It's a sign of prestige to take back European luxury goods like Gucci, Bulgari and Yves Saint Laurent. They're status symbols.

K So any package should focus on shopping opportunities.

H Definitely.

D As most of them are on a first-time visit, it's important to include visits to the cultural icons of the country, like the Tower of London or the Eiffel Tower.

H Yes, and they also want all the visitor information to be in their own language.

K Mandarin.

H Yes, but maybe some other dialects as well. It depends where they're coming from. Not everyone speaks Mandarin.

K I think there could be a big market for semi-FITs.

D Sorry, semi-FITs?

K Yes, FIT, Free Independent Traveller; so semi-FITs would probably travel with their own bilingual guide but not so much in a group.

D OK. So how could this semi-FIT market be exploited?

K I think there's a kind of missing link between supply and demand. There's a growing demand in China – we know that – but the major Chinese operators are still focusing exclusively on the mass market, on getting volume business and not enough on what the Generation Y people really want. I think there's real potential for operators like Qù Tours to focus on the high-spending customer. They may not

have so many customers but, in fact, they'll earn more money per customer and they'll be able to build up a brand image based on quality. And we can provide that quality service from our end.

H Sounds good. I like the idea of tapping into that market but let's not forget that most high-spending tourism comes from business travel and official delegations.

K Sure. OK, let's now decide how we're going to respond to that email from Huang Meng …

Unit 2

2.1

B = Brad, K = Kristin

B So, has the web designer got it up and running? Is it online?

K I'm trying out the beta version now. This is the URL: http, colon, double slash, www, dot, transfare, dot, com.

B It's taking an awfully long time to load … OK, there are lots of images slowly coming up now.

K Maybe this is a slow connection. Or we don't have enough bandwidth. No, the images are probably too big. Look at the size of that plane! OK, here we are. It says, 'Skip intro'.

B Why is there an introduction?

K Search me! I don't know. OK, here we are – here's the home page.

B Wow! Look at all those different colours! All the headers are in different colours. It looks awful – the layout's terrible! And there are too many fonts and font sizes.

K Yeah, it's gross! All right, let's try a drop-down menu. Where's the cursor gone? Oh, here we are: 'About us'.

B There's an enormous amount of text to read; I'm not sure I'd want to scroll down all that. Look, there's a link to a video – try clicking on that.

K Where?

B There.

K I can't see a link. Oh, OK. Right, it's loading now.

B It's taking its time!

K 'Play'. Nothing's happening.

B It's stuck. Click on the 'Back' button of the browser and we'll have a look at another page.

K OK. What's this? 'Internet Explorer cannot display the webpage.'

B OK, get out of it and we'll try again.

K I can't. The program's crashed. I'll have to boot up the computer again.

2.2

I = Interviewer, M = Mark Scholl

I Mark Scholl, you were involved in the famous *The best job in the world* campaign and back then many people were saying that advertising no longer works, and that the best thing was to stop wasting money on advertising and put one's faith in social media. Do you think that conventional advertising is dead?

M Well, I'd say that's an exaggeration. The campaign was a success because it was an integrated marketing strategy. It included some forms of traditional advertising and a dose of social media because, well, you just can't ignore the influence of social

media sites like YouTube or Facebook. Like if Facebook were a country, it'd probably be the third biggest in the world, behind India and China. And about two-thirds of the global internet population visit social media sites.

I OK, but what about the return on investment? Can that be measured?

M Well, the first thing to remember is that using social media isn't just another form of advertising where you just deliver a message. It's not a monologue, it's a dialogue. It means establishing two-way communication and interacting with the customers. That's why during the campaign each stage was engineered so people couldn't resist talking about it and sharing it with each other. And we kept up the dialogue with them. For example, after we'd shortlisted 50 candidates, we invited people to use a wild card and vote for the best individual they'd seen. Over 475,000 votes were cast.

I The initial money set aside for the campaign was just $1.2 million. Can you quantify the benefits of the campaign? I mean, that was a pretty shoestring budget.

M Well, yes, it was, and we've estimated that the media coverage amounted to about $165 million. So, the return on investment was phenomenal and rather unexpected. The numbers are actually pretty staggering. We reached a global audience of over three billion, there were job applications from 197 countries and 34,684 one-minute videos were uploaded. At least one person from every country in the world applied. For the website we had 53,889,455 page views, with each person spending an average of 8.62 minutes on the site. I think you'll agree that's pretty impressive!

I Sure! But perhaps we should now turn to the ways in which …

2.3

Good morning, everybody and thank you for coming. Today I'm going to talk to you about how important it is to maintain and improve your website. Everybody has a website and it's a window for everybody to look through, so it's very important to make sure not only that it is attractive but also that you refresh it on a regular basis so it doesn't go stale. There are a number of ways you can do this and I'll be giving you a few ideas.

First of all, regular news releases can be a great way to bring people's attention to any recent initiatives or special offers you may have. You can create a menu for new posts that lets visitors to your site browse the topics, usually by the date when they were written. These have the added value of being recognized as updated content by search engines. I'll talk about them later.

Another way of arousing interest is by online newsletters. You can ask visitors to subscribe through an RSS feed and publish the newsletter according to a realistic schedule. They can be time-consuming to write, so perhaps you will want to outsource them to professional travel writers or involve your own staff. It is probably best to tailor the content to a specific audience and send them an email with each new issue, inviting them to click on a link to the relevant page.

An excellent way to broadcast information about your hotel or resort or destination is by a podcast. Basically, this is an audio file that your customers can listen to on their computers or MP3 players. The files can be hosted on your site's server and you can encourage customers to subscribe to your podcasts via an RSS feed, which automatically downloads the latest talk. Podcasts are perfect for guided tours, especially when delivered by means of mobile web devices and smartphones. In this case, a visitor could download a podcast to their phone and listen to a description before or while they visit your property or destination.

But perhaps even better than podcasts is the use of embedded video. It really is the perfect medium to show the world what your destination is like, broadcast interviews, show the waves breaking on the beach or the snow falling on the mountain slopes. And, of course, you can embed videos into your webpages or create your own YouTube channel.

Before I answer any questions, I should mention search engine optimization. How do you get search engines to rank your site high up the list? The most important thing is for the page code to have meta tags. These help tell search engines what your site is about. And it's important to choose meaningful headers, which the search robots will pick up as relevant.

2.4

1

A Can you see any signs for Genesis Valley?

B No, but we're on the road for Stanton.

A The website said to take a sharp right.

B But when?

C I think there was a right turn back there but we were going too fast.

2

A Shall we go into the greenhouse now? I think they've got some insect-eating plants in there.

B We saw them last year. It's boring.

A OK. Let's go into the museum. There are lots of stuffed animals in there. You'll like that.

C Can I have an ice cream?

A You know they don't sell ice creams here.

D The leaflet at the entrance says you can buy ice cream and soft drinks in the tea shop.

A There used to be a teashop but it closed down. I don't know why.

C I want an ice cream!

A Stop it.

B I'm hungry, too. I didn't have any breakfast.

D OK, be quiet, you two. We'll go out and have some lunch in Abbots Bickington. But first we'll have a look round the museum.

B Do we have to?

D Yes. Now, where is the museum? It's not on the map of the site. But I think it's up here. Come on.

3

A As you probably know, the first plausible explanation for the dance of the Apis Mellifera, commonly known as the honey bee, was posited in the 1960s by the Nobel Prize winning zoologist Karl von Frisch. He speculated that the direction to which the bees point when performing the dance indicates the direction of the food source in relation to the sun, while the intensity of the abdominal waggles indicates how far away it is. Now, the dance is generally performed near the entrance to the hive and …

B What's he on about? I don't understand a word he's saying!

C Neither do I. Let's go somewhere else.

4

A Look at these figures, Sally. Visitor numbers are down 18 percent compared to last year. We've got to do something about it. We could start with the website.

B What's wrong with the website? My husband designed it!

A We have to make it more interactive. We need to look at search engine optimization and banner advertising, email marketing and so on.

C Yes, and people get a lot of information on their smartphones as well, like a podcast of a guided tour.

B Sorry, I don't understand 'search engine optimization' or 'podcasts'. In my day, you just went to the local Visitor Information Centre and picked up a leaflet!

A Well, that's not good enough these days. We need to define who our customers are, target them and get them to come back again with new events and attractions.

C I agree. We need to move with the times.

B All right. John, can you get in touch with a media consultant and ask them to prepare a report for the next board meeting?

A Will do. I know a very good one called Anita Drysdale.

Unit 3

3.1

OK, everybody. Well, that was very interesting. Most of you seem to have identified the essential difference: basically, a product is a fabricated article or a good that benefits the user in some way. It could even be a food item, like a hamburger. And one hamburger is much the same as another hamburger. Whereas a brand is an identity which adds value and makes a product or service different from the competition. My name is Martina McDonald and I have nothing to do with hamburgers but the name McDonald's is a good example of a brand: it has an image, not just in the sense of a visual image – the Golden Arches logo – but as a concept involving family, fast service, value for money and consistently reliable quality. And the McDonald's concept is recognized globally from Barcelona to Beijing. Are we all clear about that?

3.2

A What about branding in the hotel industry?

B Well, if the hotel room is the same size and the bed as big or comfortable, there's no way of telling one hotel from another except price. But competing on price isn't a good strategy in the hospitality industry, so hotels have to distinguish themselves from their competitors and tailor what they offer to the expectations, budget and travel needs of their guests. Through advertising and marketing they need to create brand awareness so that potential guests easily recognize the name of the hotel. They have to build up a brand image so that people can easily identify with them and know exactly what to expect when they arrive. They also try to create brand loyalty so guests will keep coming back, not because the hotel is cheaper – it may be more expensive – but because they remain faithful to that organization, they trust it to deliver the same level of service each time.

3.3

1 I enjoy travelling but checking into a hotel isn't always the most pleasant experience. Many of the rooms are as small as a shoebox, lacking in character and totally depressing. But in the very near future chances are that the design of a typical hotel room will be very different. Scientists at a research centre in Germany have built a revolutionary hotel room to show the hotel industry how they can use new technology to make rooms more inspiring. First of all, the configuration will change: unlike the rectangular shoebox, there will be no straight lines – everything will be round. Why? Because research has shown that curves and rounded surfaces are best at putting people at ease.

2 In all probability, there'll be a voice-activated computer on the wall, through which you can find out what time breakfast is, find out about the hotel's services, watch a video on demand or even ask it to gently rock your bed as you fall asleep.

3 I think that for the next generation of guests it's highly likely that they'll be able to choose the décor of the room from a whole rainbow of colours just by pressing a button. So, you don't have to lie on your back in bed and look at something white if you prefer a shade of red, blue, green or whatever colour you choose.

4 The next time you stay in a hotel and have to get up in the middle of the night, you may not need to switch on the light because the light may well come on for you. They'll be equipped with sensors that detect your presence and turn the lights on automatically. Press a button and you'll get a scented aroma. And that's not all! There's bound to be a jacuzzi and there could even be a television for you to watch as you lie back and soak.

5 What about this? Flick a switch and the view outside turns into a gigantic video screen. Flick it back and look at the flowers in the garden. The only problem is that once you've checked into the hotel, you probably won't want to check out!

3.4

S = Sally, M = Michael, A = Financial Advisor

S My parents died recently and we've inherited a large house. We both have some savings, so we thought we would like to open a bed and breakfast. In fact, this is something we've been planning to do for some time.

M We've brought this table for you to look at with an idea of our start-up costs. We've done our homework and had some estimates from various people. The property does need some renovation – rewiring the electricity, plumbing, painting, that kind of thing – so we've contacted builders, gardeners and so on and we expect that will be a one-off fixed cost of $22,200.

A Yes, and I see you've very sensibly broken that down into an annual and monthly cost so you can see what your long-term overheads are.

S And then we've estimated the price of bedding – mattresses, sheets, blankets, that kind of thing – and that's $4,500. In all likelihood, that will have to be renewed after five years.

M We've decided to buy the best for the kitchen equipment and we've also had to include smoke detectors to comply with the health and safety legislation.

A I'm surprised at the cost of the road signs and front entrance sign! Do they really cost $2,000?

M Well, that's what we were quoted. Maybe we could look at that again.

A And then there are the legal fees – the costs of permits and licences. That's an initial fixed cost of $1,200.

S Yes. And $2,400 for advertising and promotion for the first year of operation.

A OK, so the grand total is $34,100. Of course, there are things like depreciation which you need to take into consideration but your accountant will be able to explain that to you.

3.5

S = Sally, A = Financial Advisor, M = Michael

S What we're not sure about is how to calculate the room rate.

A How many rooms do you plan to have?

S Four.

A OK. Well, it depends on your rate of occupancy – how many bed nights you can sell. Let's take the worst-case scenario. You have start-up costs for the first year of $34,100; and let's say, for the sake of argument, that you want a return on your investment of $25,900 in the first year. That makes a total target sale of bed nights of $60,000 but you only manage to sell 300 bed nights. So you would have to charge $60,000 divided by 300, which is $200. Obviously, that might be too much but it depends on the quality of the accommodation and the competition. Let's take a better scenario, where you sold 1,000 bed nights – that's an occupancy rate of about 60 percent; then you would charge $60,000 divided by 1,000, which equals $60, which makes you very competitive.

M That sounds very reasonable.

3.6

D = Dave, T = Teresa, S = Sarah

D Teresa, which property do you think is the best bet?

T Well, I like the place in South Dakota.

D But it's a franchise.

T I know it's a franchise, which means that we don't own it, the hotel chain does, but we benefit from the brand name and get help with training, advertising and promotion. We've never owned or run a property before and we need professional advice.

S OK, but isn't it better to own the motel? Then we could always sell it if it doesn't work out.

T Maybe. Anyway, I've been doing some sums: if we have 90 percent occupancy for the high season and charge $100 a night, and 30 percent occupancy off-season at, say, $70 a night, that makes a turnover of $360,000 plus $46,000.

D So total sales would be $406,000.

T Yes, give or take a few thousand. And I've calculated that the total cost for food and beverage, telephone, advertising, insurance and everything else would give us a profit of about $150,000 a year.

S OK, but it does say there's some need for refurbishment. That would be an extra cost, wouldn't it?

T Sure, but the bank loan would cover that, wouldn't it? What do you think, Dave?

D You've forgotten the upfront fee and the royalty we'd have to pay. And I'm not convinced your figures are right – it sounds very complicated. But anyway, we don't have to decide anything yet.

T OK, so what takes your fancy?

D Personally, I prefer Estonia. It's a much more interesting place than South Dakota and I've been told that it's the only hotel on the island, so it's got no competition. We'd be guaranteed reservations.

T That depends if anyone goes there. After all, it's on an island. How would people get there? Is there a regular ferry service? We don't know.

D I'd much prefer to live there than in the United States and it's got great potential. It's cheaper, so we wouldn't need to borrow so much from the bank to expand.

T OK, but we don't know the operating costs.

D Well, I emailed the owners and the average daily rate seems to be about $150 a night – $175 in high season and $125 in low season. They say there's an occupancy rate of 75 percent peak season and 35 percent low season. And on a turnover of $420,000 they manage to make a pre-tax profit of $115,000.

T Sarah, I suppose you prefer the place in Mallorca?

S Actually, I do. I think we could get a very good price if we bargained hard. And I really like the idea of only working eight months a year!

D Why only eight months?

S Apparently, until recently it was fully booked during that period and they just shut it down low season.

T Yes, but how many guests would we get if the market's now gone into decline? And don't forget we'd have to live somewhere. That's a cost too.

S We could live in the hotel rent-free! OK, I rang up the owners. Apparently, they're selling for health reasons and they say that with an average daily rate of $155 and an occupancy of 95 percent for the season, they managed to turn over $265,000 last year. So the place brought in a profit of around $90,000–100,000 net. That's still pretty good.

D OK. So what I suggest is that we discuss the pros and cons in more detail and that each of us goes away and writes a short business plan. Then we can perhaps come to some sort of decision.

Unit 4

4.1

1 We've been here since the beginning of the 1990s, when tourism really began to take off, and it is one of the best places for a beach holiday. Goa's relatively free from crime and there's a fantastic nightlife. Every year we're fully booked and our profits have gone up year on year, so you can imagine our shareholders back home are delighted. And very soon we'll be creating a luxury golf course and a spa and wellness centre so that'll be another source of revenue. You know, some people say we don't do enough for the local community but all the food we serve in the resort is bought from local farmers, so I don't really see the objection.

2 Every day I'm working ten-hour shifts as a chambermaid in a hotel which is owned by a foreign investment company. I have two children and my husband is dead, so I am very poor. We are thinking every day what we're going to eat and how to pay for the electricity and the rent. I have to go to work every day thinking of all of this. I have to smile to the tourists but it is not what I am feeling in my soul. I do not get paid when I am working overtime or taking my holidays. I would like to join a trade union to help fight for better pay and conditions but the hotel won't allow it.

3 There is a growing discontent with the way tourism has developed in Goa. The income derived from tourism has not been distributed fairly and several demonstrations have been held in protest. There have been disputes over the use of state-owned bus companies rather than local auto rickshaws and the employment of overseas resort representatives rather than local people who could do the job just as well or better.

4 I spend my day selling ice creams and sweets and I can earn enough money to survive the monsoon season, when there are very few tourists. But then I have to go back to my village and help on my father's farm. I prefer working here because the tourists are rich, give me tips and I can go to beach parties and meet lots of different people I wouldn't normally meet. But I don't know what will happen next year because the authorities are banning people like me and the owners of market stalls along the seafront. They say we are too poor and harass the tourists but it's not true.

4.2

The Galapagos islands have an official name, the Archipélago de Colón, in honour of the Italian navigator Christopher Columbus. This Spanish name dates back to 1892, when the world was celebrating the 400th anniversary of Christopher Columbus' famous voyage of discovery. But, in fact, Columbus never sailed anywhere near the islands. The Galapagos only became famous after the publication of Darwin's book *On the Origin of Species*. His observations and collections of the wildlife on the islands led to his theory of evolution by natural selection.

The islands are located around the equator in the Pacific Ocean, about 1,000 kilometres west of Ecuador, and form one of that country's 24 provinces.

The Galapagos population has increased over 300 percent in the past few decades and the population is doubling every eleven years. People from mainland Ecuador have literally invaded the islands, hoping to find work. Today more than 40,000 people live on the islands and the population could reach 65,000 by the end of the decade.

Visitor numbers, which have risen from 41,000 20 years ago, are now more than 160,000 a year and are expected to reach 180,000 in the next couple of years.

There is an astonishing variety of wildlife in the Galapagos – the iguanas and turtles are perhaps the most famous. But did you know that there is also a Galapagos penguin? It's the only penguin that lives on the equator in the wild.

4.3

A Thank you, Lewis, for your mail and I think you make some very valid points. Could I start by just reminding everyone that, in fact, visitor numbers to the islands are strictly controlled. The number of people coming ashore, how long they stay and the places they visit are all monitored. For the past 14 years they've been mainly concentrated on the three islands of Isabela, Santa Cruz and San Cristobal. And I should also point out that the number of sites that can be visited is limited and all excursions have to be accompanied by a certified guide.

B OK, I agree that these arrangements have been positive but at present we welcome about 160,000 visitors a year and that number should now be an absolute limit. I don't want to sound alarming but the present situation is unsustainable and we really need to do something to protect these islands before it's too late.

C I must say I agree with Lewis. Recently we had an invasion of rats brought in by one of the ships in the port. I haven't got the details with me but I'll bring a report for our next meeting on how we're treating the problem.

D As a representative of the Santa Cruz Pleasure Boats, I really don't think the rat problem is important. It's just an isolated case and certainly nothing to do with us. But what I would say is that the number of luxury pleasure boats should be cut. There

are far too many operators and they're taking away local trade not only from us but local guest houses as well. In fact, only 15 percent of income from tourism ends up in our pockets – the rest just leaks away.

4.4

F = Fernando Morales, B = Barbara White, R = Richard Baxter, H = Dr Howard, T = Tanya Olsen

F Good morning, everybody. Good morning, everybody. I think we're all here now, so shall we get started? I'm sorry I wasn't able to circulate an agenda as this meeting is being held at such short notice. So, the reason I've called this meeting is to discuss the accident last Thursday and how we can avoid such accidents in the future. I'd like to invite all your comments on this incident. Um, Barbara, can you give us an update?

B Thank you. As you know, the cruise ship *MS Discovery* sank after hitting an iceberg. An Australian vessel went to the rescue and, apparently, the operation went smoothly and now all 285 passengers and crew have been safely flown back to mainland Chile.

R No, it didn't go smoothly! It took three and a half hours for the sister ship to arrive, which is far too long!

F Right. Thank you, Richard. Does anyone have anything to add to that? Doctor Howard, would you like to say something?

H Yes, if a similar incident were to happen off the Australian Antarctic territory, a rescue ship would not necessarily be so close at hand. The distances to the Antarctic from Australia are much greater and the sea is much rougher. So, because of the extreme conditions that can be faced out there, the management of tourism in east Antarctica is actually even more problematic than in the peninsula.

T I think it's really terrible to think that the ship is at the bottom of the sea in 500 metres of icy water. Is there any way the ship can be refloated before it starts leaking oil?

F Tanya, that's an important question but can we stick to the point under discussion: how can such accidents be avoided? Does anyone want to come in here? Barbara?

B Well, all boats should be equipped with both forward- and downward-looking sonar to listen out for sounds generated by passing ships, submarines, icebergs and any uncharted rocks underwater. If the *MS Discovery* had had sonar, this might not have happened.

H Can I make a point here? Sonar is fine but it can interfere with marine animals that use echolocation and when a number of ships are in the same area, they can interfere with each other.

T I'd like to raise the subject of lifeboats. Apparently, the lifeboats in the rescue operation were uncovered and the passengers had to wait for several hours in freezing conditions. I suggest all lifeboats should be covered.

F Good point. Perhaps we could come back to that later, Tanya? I've put safety and security as item three on the agenda.

H I understand the crew was extremely

professional but it does highlight the need for all crews to be highly trained in this kind of operation.

R I personally think tourism is getting out of hand. Very few of the new ships sailing south this year have strengthened hulls to protect them against icebergs and frozen seawater. Some of the ships carry 6,000 passengers, which is far too many. They produce an average of 3.5 kilograms of garbage per person per day. Much of this waste is not easily biodegradable and some will inevitably end up on the ocean floor.

T Yes, Richard's right. And in the past few years there have been court cases against cruise ship companies who have been found guilty of discharging oil and polluting the waters with waste chemicals. In one case, a company was fined 18 million dollars. These cruise ships should be banned.

F I'm sorry, we don't have much time and we really must keep to the agenda. OK, are there any further points anyone wants to raise? No? OK, let's move on to the next item on the agenda, which is …

4.5

I = Interviewer, T = Tourist Board representative, M = Mayor, W = Croatian Wildlife Association representative

I So, as I understand it, the Board of Tourism is now planning to develop a different kind of tourism experience for these islands and that would involve the development of a new eco-resort on the island of Mali Brijun.

T Yes, and it's a very exciting idea. As you know, the island has a great deal to offer. A lot of famous people have stayed there and the facilities are first-class. But we now want to diversify and attract tourists to a more back-to-nature kind of tourism, which will allow people to enjoy themselves but in harmony with the natural world.

I It's certainly a beautiful place and I was fascinated to learn that there are over 200 dinosaur footprints on the island!

T Yes, and we're thinking of creating a dinosaur park on the island. We already have a number of international investors interested in the project.

I But won't this development actually pose a threat to the environment with an influx of tourists who may or may not be responsible and respectful of the environment?

M Well, this is an ambitious project but we will have to strike a balance between the needs of the tourists and protection of the eco-system. Some of the endangered species on Veliki Brijun grow freely on the island of Mali Brijun, for example, the wild cucumber and some species of grass. There are some very old trees as well. I should also say that 80 percent of the protected area of the National Park is, in fact, under water – there are many types of fish that live in the waters around Mali Brijun and, of course, the turtles and the pink dolphins. So, protecting the environment is our main priority but we also have to balance that against the opportunity to benefit from the revenue that tourism brings.

I And what's the position of the Wildlife Association?

W This whole project is absolutely absurd! What are we really talking about? The construction of roads and footpaths through the forest, accommodation with hot water, electricity and parking spaces for these so-called ecotourists, water sports which will inevitably have an impact on the marine life. We don't need this project – it won't even create jobs.

T That's not true; there will be at least 75 jobs and every attempt will be made to safeguard the environment. Why would we want to destroy the attraction that we want people to come and enjoy?

M Yes, though I'm not sure that all of these jobs will be permanent. And we must make sure that the money generated does not all leak away to foreign tour operators. I don't think our local people would be happy about that.

T There's absolutely no need to worry. We can levy an eco-tax on tourism in the archipelago; that should provide enough money for the local community to spend on whatever projects they decide – for schools, adult training initiatives, clinics and hospitals, whatever they want.

I Well, I see there are still a number of issues to discuss and it will be interesting to learn more about the development in a future programme. Thank you for giving us your views. And that's all from me, so back to the studio …

Unit 5

5.1

1 I think they should make it easy for people to orientate themselves and get where they want to go more easily. Airports are big places and it's easy to lose sense of direction, so passengers need to know where to go. It helps if there are pictograms for services that can easily be represented by a visual icon like taxis, phones, wheelchair access, that kind of thing.

2 There are lines for check-in, then passport control, security, the departure gate, then your seat on the aircraft and baggage claim and immigration at the other end. It's appalling! Why don't they employ enough staff?

3 I hate walking along corridors and enclosed areas with lots of advertisements on the walls as these can be very visually tiring and create additional stress. I'd like to travel through airports with open spaces and light glass walls that give a view of the planes on the tarmac. The whole place should feel airy and unconstrained.

4 I personally don't drive as there's a lot of congestion on the access roads and the long-term car park is quite a distance from the terminal building. They should think more about the design of the landside areas because you often feel you're in the middle of nowhere and it's very disorienting.

5.2

R = Rachel, K = Karen, S = Steve, C = Clare

R OK, this is just a short meeting to discuss some of the difficult situations you've had to face recently and how well you were able to deal with them. Karen, would you like to start the ball rolling?

K Sure. Recently I had to check in an extended family group going off together for a family holiday – maybe fourteen children – the parents were totally overwhelmed with the kids crawling on the floor and others trying to run away. When I asked for the passports, there was a row between the parents about who had whose passport, they started opening all their baggage on the floor, everything was spread around and then other passengers in the queue started to get annoyed and abusive.

R So how did you deal with it?

K I had to take the family away from the other passengers and I asked Dalal to open another counter to finish the check-in. The family finally managed to present all the required documents but not in time, and they had to wait another two hours to get on the next flight to Madrid.

R What about you, Steve?

S I had a situation yesterday because of a late check-in. A guy came running up to my check-in desk and said, all out of breath, 'Please, please … traffic jam! It's impossible to drive here! Please, I must be on that flight, please!' The check-in had closed 25 minutes before and I really didn't see a solution. But then he told me his story and why he was in such a panic. His wife was in labour and she was in the ambulance on her way to the hospital.

R OK. So, was he allowed on the flight?

S Yes, I called the captain and he agreed to let him on board and, apparently, shortly afterwards there was an announcement on board congratulating him on the birth of his first child.

C Rachel, can you tell us about what happened to Tadzio? None of us was on duty that day and we haven't seen him since.

R Well, I don't know if you know the full story but Justyna was on duty and a passenger became very abusive with her and then hit her in the face! Tadzio was on the next counter and although I understand his behaviour, I don't approve of it. He got up, punched the man on the nose and then apparently said, 'I'm really sorry for the inconvenience but I suggest you now queue at another counter as I'm quite likely to be fired. It's been a pleasure to work for this company. Goodbye.' Anyway, that's what he told me.

C So, has he got the sack?

R No, but he's been disciplined and suspended for two weeks. We actually received letters of support from the passengers who witnessed the incident and Justyna has received an apology from the passenger who hit her. But he has now been blacklisted and won't be able to fly with us for at least three years.

5.3

S = Supervisor, A = Customer service Agent, P1 = Passenger 1, P2 = Passenger 2, P3 = Passenger 3

S I'm afraid you'll have to tell the passengers waiting at Gate 24 that the flight to Frankfurt has been cancelled. There are no flights until tomorrow morning. Sorry.

A Another cancellation! But these guys have been waiting here since about ten o'clock this morning and it's now half past four! This has got to be the worst day I've ever had here! OK, thank you, I'll break the news. Can I have your attention, please? I'd like to inform all passengers to Frankfurt that, due to a cancellation, there are unfortunately now no more seats available until tomorrow morning.

P1 We've been waiting here all day. What I want to know is whether you'll be refunding the transfers at the other end.

A I can't tell you that.

P1 And the hotel?

A I can't say that.

P2 Why can't you?

A I'm sorry. I fully understand how you feel.

P2 No, you don't understand at all!

A I can understand why you're feeling frustrated but I'm afraid I don't have that information.

P2 Well, get it!

A We don't have that information.

P2 What do you mean? Someone must have it!

A I'm very sorry, I hear what you're saying but I'm not at the present time able to help you. There's a complaints procedure in place and what we recommend …

P3 Listen, mate, that is just not acceptable! You're a waste of space!

A Sorry, sir, I think you should calm down now. Could you just tone down your language, please?

P3 Are you going to get me to Frankfurt this evening?

A I can't.

P3 Why not?

A I'm very sorry for the inconvenience but there are no more seats.

P3 Why not?

A There are no more seats.

P3 Why not? I want an answer!

A I have no control over the situation. I'm just passing on information. But I'll tell you what I can do. I can put you on a flight to Munich this evening. There are still seats on the Munich flight leaving at 21.25.

P1 That's no good to me! Are you telling me that you can get us to Munich but it's impossible to get us to Frankfurt 250 miles away? It's the same country, isn't it? Or have they got a totally different climate down south?

A I'm very sorry, sir. I'm doing my best to help you but that's all I can do for you at this moment in time.

5.4

P1 We've been waiting here all day. What I want to know is whether you'll be refunding the transfers at the other end.

A There's no problem, everything will be taken care of and we will give you a form to fill in so that you will be reimbursed.

P1 And the hotel?

A Yes, you'll also be able to claim for the hotel room.

P2 From you or the hotel?

A It's OK, there's no need to worry. The airline will meet all your extra expenses.

P3 Are you going to get me to Frankfurt this evening?

A I fully understand how you feel but I'm afraid it doesn't look as if that's going to be possible.

P3 Why not?

A I'm very sorry for the inconvenience but there are no more seats.

P3 Why not?

A Well, unfortunately, I've been told that there are no more seats. So, I'm afraid it's not going to be possible.

P3 Why not? I want an answer!

A I hear what you're saying but, honestly, I have no control over the situation. I'm just passing on information. But I'll tell you what I can do …

5.5

RAA1 = Regional Airport Authority Representative 1, RAA2 = Regional Airport Authority Representative 2, BL1 = BeeLines Representative 1, BL2 = Beelines Representative 2

RAA1 Well, I think there are serious safety and security issues. Probably the most important at the moment is congestion and delays, so we have a problem with incoming aircraft having to circle overhead and wait in sequence before they can land. That's dangerous as planes could easily run out of fuel if they have to wait too long.

RAA2 Yes, and the runway is only 1,670 metres and the taxiway is too short. We need to increase capacity and attract more frequent flights, shorter turnaround times and more passengers. Then we'd be able to boost revenue through more scheduled slots and landing fees.

RAA1 That's all very well and we need more capital because otherwise we can't meet infrastructure costs. But the airport simply can't handle the number of passengers that we have at the present time. The long lines at check-in are unmanageable and it takes far too long to get through security. We get a lot of angry people and a lot of abuse both on and off the planes.

RAA2 What about self-service check-in kiosks? Wouldn't they speed things up?

BL1 We were planning to install these but, apparently, there's some kind of objection because they help criminals get onto flights without any kind of ID verification.

RAA1 Don't you have personnel walking the line and pulling out people who need to check in for flights leaving soon?

BL1 I wish we did but we have staffing problems too. Sometimes there just aren't enough people to go round. They can't be in two places at the same time.

RAA2 What other problems come to mind?

BL2 Parking. There are too few spaces and too many cars.

BL1 Traffic. People miss their flights because there isn't a fast rail link to the airport and buses and private cars get stuck in traffic.

BL2 Facilities. There aren't enough seats in the lounges; we don't make any attempt to maximize revenue through the rental of more retail outlets in the terminal because there isn't enough space.

RAA1 OK, that's enough for the moment. I suggest we go away and think more about the issues and how we can develop this airport. Then come back in a week's time and hold another meeting. Are we all agreed? OK. If you can get your ideas to me between now and then, I'll circulate an agenda before we meet.

Unit 6

6.1

During the 18th century Pompeii figured on the Grand Tour of Europe and the sons of many of the noble and rich families used to visit Pompeii as well as Rome and Venice. Many European countries, thanks to the new importance given to the ancient world, opened academies in Naples and Rome to offer hospitality to those who wanted to study the newly excavated towns. Given the enthusiasm for all things Italian, visitors would commission artists to paint original works, landscapes and city views. They would then take them back home as souvenirs or gifts for family and friends.

All of the paintings are of animals such as deer that the cave dwellers used to see all around them. We don't know why they painted them but it is often said that they may well have had some magic significance and meant to increase the number of animals. I personally doubt this but it is also believed that they had been painted by shamans who could talk to spirits of animals. They would retreat to the back of the cave, go into a trance and paint their visions, perhaps to make it easier to capture the animals.

6.2

S = Sonia, T = Tourist

S OK, everyone. Can everyone hear? Yes? I suggest all the children come to the front so they can see better. Right, we're now in the Gold Drawing Room, which, as you can see, deserves its name because everything here is gilded and elaborately decorated – the vaulted ceilings, the doors, the gold-plated chandeliers and the period furniture. And if you look along the walls, you can see the massive rectangular columns embellished with finely-wrought ornate patterns in Byzantine style; and on either side of the room a couple of elegant vases. The furniture in this room was designed by a cabinet maker in Moscow.

T Is this the original decoration?

S No. In fact, this room was reconstructed following the fire of 1837 by the architect Alexander Brullov, who also designed the Malachite Room we saw earlier. But what you see here is the original decoration.

T OK, thanks.

S Right. This room was used by Tsarina Maria Alexandrovna as a state drawing room following her marriage in 1841 to Alexander II. When Alexander was 20, he toured Europe in search of a wife and was at one time interested in Queen Victoria of England but Victoria married her German cousin, Albert of Saxe-Coburg. Then Alexander fell in love with princess Marie of Hesse, who was just 14 years old. His mother was against the marriage, not because of her age but because she was illegitimate. So she became the Empress Maria Alexandrovna and is said to have been shy, with no taste in fashion, no interesting conversation and no charm. She was often sick and the damp climate of St Petersburg did not agree with her chest infection but she was sufficiently healthy to have eight children, six boys and two girls, five of whom continued the family line. OK, now why don't we retrace our steps back to the main staircase and head towards …

6.3

First of all, if you want to be a good guide, you have to have a number of skills and personal qualities. Let's begin with the personal qualities. You have to like working with and for other people – that means being friendly and helpful at all times and knowing what to do in unexpected circumstances, for example, if the building has to be evacuated or someone is taken ill. You have to be enthusiastic, good-humoured and as in many ways it's a performance – you're an entertainer – you need to have an outgoing personality. What else? It's important not to get impatient if someone asks a thousand questions or tries to contradict you. And as you're likely to be on your feet and walking up and down stairs all day, you need to be fit and have plenty of stamina. But not all the people in your party will be as fit as you, so you should be sensitive to the group's needs and limitations. For example, if there are elderly people in your group, don't expect them to walk fast.

Of course, you have to have a great deal of background knowledge. You need to do your research beforehand and have all the facts, dates and details at your fingertips. On the other hand, people are on holiday and should be having fun, not just being given a constant stream of facts, so you should also make an attempt to be as entertaining as possible. Make the place come alive by telling anecdotes about strange or interesting things that happened there. Whenever possible, pass on any interesting information even if it's not immediately relevant.

Guiding is all about communication, so you should speak in a loud and clear voice. Don't go too fast or too slow. And don't forget that communication is not just about how you speak and get your message across; it's also about making good eye contact and using the right body language. OK, well, now I'm going to …

6.4

1 The tower is one thousand three hundred and forty-six feet tall.

2 The city was under siege from nineteen forty-one to nineteen forty-three.

3 The antechamber measures fifteen metres by thirty-five metres.

4 The lake formed approximately two hundred and fifty thousand years ago.

5 The splendid Kolyvan Vase is two point five seven metres high.

6 The west wing was opened in two thousand and one.

7 The parquet floor is three quarters of an inch thick.

8 She was born on the sixth of January, fifteen forty-six.

9 There are over seventy-five million visitors.

10 The guide book costs just sixteen dollars ninety.

11 The statue dates back to the second century BCE.

12 St Petersburg is the second largest city in Russia. The population is four million, nine hundred and fifty-four thousand.

6.5

C = Curator, I = Interior Designer, A = Albert Johnson

C I must say we've been very lucky to receive this collection and thank you for giving us an inventory. So, what we have to do now is decide how we can sort the exhibits according to different criteria and display them in some sort of logical order in the space that we have.

I Yes, but, possibly, the first thing we have to do is to give visitors some background information about Ascoby Hall. Can you tell us anything about that, Mr Johnson?

A Yes, well, I'm a direct descendant of Geoffrey Johnson, who first built the house in 1399.

C What was the original layout of the house?

A The west wing was the area where the family used to live and the other wing was for the servants and the kitchen area. And the entrance used to be the main hall where the family would eat and entertain. Then the house was handed down from generation to generation and, although we don't know for sure, Tobias Johnson is said to have installed the magnificent stained glass window overlooking the courtyard.

C Yes, and he was the man who founded the Gentlemen's Society in 1747. As I understand it, the members would meet every month and discuss all sorts of topical issues. The great mathematical genius Isaac Newton, who wrote one of the most important works in the history of science, *Principia Mathematica*, was a member and so was Matthew Flinders.

A That's right. He was the man who first sailed round Australia.

I So, looking at the floor plan, we basically have an entrance area and eight rooms of different sizes. I think we need to have a room about the house itself and another room dedicated to the Gentlemen's Society.

C Yes, I think so.

I What about having a room about the geography of the local area?

A Yes, well, as you know, most of the land round here is very flat and was just a swampy marsh until Dutch engineers came over in the 17th century to reclaim the land from the sea.

C That's why the area is known as South Holland.

I And we could have a room for local history. We could include information about the Roman conquest of Britain and the Saxon and Viking invasions.

A Yes, and perhaps another room about local places of interest that have some connection with those periods. For example, a lot of the place names around here have definite Saxon or Viking origins.

C OK. But what else? That's only five rooms so far. Have you got any other ideas?

Unit 7

7.1

I = Interviewer, E = Emma Murray

I So, Emma Murray, you're the events co-ordinator for a major football club. Can you tell us how you got the job in the first place?

E Well, when I did a degree in Travel and Tourism at Birmingham City University. I didn't specialize in Events Management but during my studies, I realized that this was an area I was particularly interested in. I did my third year work placement here and enjoyed it a lot. When I graduated, the club got in touch with me and asked me if I wanted to come back and work here.

I So what exactly do you do?

E I don't just put on events for the club – although that's part of it. What I do is stage events for other people using the club's facilities. We have a large number of meeting rooms and suites, so what happens is that companies and organizations can offer our hospitality and catering packages to their corporate clients before the match and, of course, they have a sensational view of the players on the pitch. We also have private executive boxes where people can entertain their guests and do business at the same time. And if anyone wants to mark a special occasion like a product launch or hold a private party, they can use the club as a venue.

I So I suppose you have to work on Saturdays?

E I work nine to five Monday to Friday and have to be present at home games, which are often on Saturdays. When I'm in the corporate hospitality suite, I have to greet the people arriving and make sure they're well looked after. You need to be confident and you need to smile – you can't have a sad face because that's not what they've paid for! But the real work is beforehand: making sure the transport arrangements are in place for people coming to the club, setting up the rooms, supervising the food preparation and seeing to any last-minute issues.

I What kind of issues?

E Recently we had a problem with a client who had invited a group of Chinese associates to watch a match, unaware of the fact that none of them spoke English fluently. If I had known about this in advance, I would have arranged for an interpreter. In the end, I managed to get in touch with someone who was willing to come and do the job but she spoke a different dialect. Another time one of the conference speakers had written the wrong date in his diary and if I hadn't confirmed with him the day before, we wouldn't have been able to find a replacement.

I You had a problem last week, didn't you?

E Yes! The match was called off 15 minutes before the game was due to start because the pitch was frozen. I thought the referee made the wrong decision but if I hadn't anticipated the bad weather, I wouldn't have had a contingency plan. Luckily, I had some alternative entertainment prepared just in case they decided to postpone or cancel the game.

I What was it?

E We watched a replay of the World Cup final on a huge high-definition screen. It wasn't the same kind of experience as a live match but I think everyone enjoyed seeing it again.

7.2

I = Interviewer, H = Hamza Habri

I Hamza, you've been organizing this festival for many years now. Can you tell us how you go about organizing a festival like this?

H Yes, well, as you know, the Gnawa festival has been held every year in Essaouira since 1998. I think that for every major event like this one, if it is going to be a success, you need a vision and a mission statement. You need to answer the question, 'Why is this event being held?' So, for us, the mission is to showcase Gnawa music and dance and to celebrate the traditions and beliefs of Morocco's Gnawa people.

I Who are the Gnawa people?

H The Gnawa of Morocco were originally black slaves who, over time, obtained their freedom. Historians believe that the Gnawa population originated from black West Africa – from Senegal and Chad and from Mali in the north to Nigeria in the south.

I OK. So, second question: who are the stakeholders in the event?

H There are many different stakeholders. First of all, the host community because there were over 450,000 visitors last year, with a large number of people coming from abroad. So, the Ministry of Tourism is involved in programming the event and liaises with the town of Essaouira. The festival obviously brings in a lot of money, so anyone involved in catering – the people manning the stalls in the fish market, the hoteliers, the people providing bed and breakfast accommodation – all these stand to gain. And with the number of overseas visitors, the airlines benefit, particularly Royal Air Maroc, as do companies like Songlines Music Travel in the UK, who organize tours to the festival and possibly a stay in Marrakech or Agadir. And I mustn't forget our main sponsor, the BMCE Bank, which backs the festival financially.

I When is the festival held?

H Yes, that's the third question: when will the event take place? Our festival takes place over four days every summer at the end of June. And the fourth question is: where exactly will it be staged? And obviously it's here in Essaouira.

I I suppose it must be quite complicated from a logistical point of view.

H Well, yes, there are so many things to coordinate and it involves a great deal of forward planning: transport of artists and their equipment, emergency and first aid access, crowd control, managing the media, supplies of food and drink, waste removal. One of the hardest things about logistics is looking at a list and spotting what is not there.

I And, finally, what is there to see and do?

H Essaouira is a relatively small town, so there are ten different concert sites with their own stages and tents for the performing musicians. The festival is also a World Music Festival, so people can choose which site to go to according to the type of music they prefer, from contemporary Moroccan music to jazz to electronic fusion.

I And apart from the music?

H If you want to take a break from the music, you can explore the backstreets of the medina, climb the ramparts of the old Portuguese town, stroll along the fishing harbour or relax on the beaches outside the town. I can assure you, you won't get bored!

7.3

I = Interviewer, H = Hamza Habri

I You talked earlier about the vision and mission statement. How do you actually translate these into objectives when you're planning the festival?

H Well, once you know what an event is designed to achieve, you can think of the objectives in terms of several key features; these are summed up in the acronym SMART.

I What does that mean?

H *S* stands for 'specific'. For example, one objective of the festival might be to attract 50,000 more people to the festival compared to last year. In fact, we now get about half a million visitors, so we've achieved that. *M* stands for 'measurable', so as I just said, an increase in the number of tickets sold can be measured, whereas an objective like 'raising awareness of Gnawa music' is less tangible.

I Right. And *A*?

H *A* means 'achievable'. There's no point in setting an objective which can't be met because it's unrealistic – for example, if we were to say that we wanted people from every country in the world to participate. *R* stands for 'relevant', so we make sure the music is basically world music and we wouldn't invite mega rock stars like Coldplay, for example. And *T* means 'time-specific'. We have to make sure that everything is on track during the planning stage and that we get our schedules right so that everything is in place by the third week of June at the very latest.

7.4

I = Interviewer, N = Nick Ikin

I Nick, I know the festival is under threat and your sponsor has threatened to pull out. I was wondering if any of the major record labels would be interested in putting up the money.

N No way! The record industry is just a corpse but there are many interesting things crawling out of it. You know, when I started, a record company wouldn't sign you unless you could generate at least 150,000 US dollars in sales but now all you need is some basic equipment to cut a CD and post it on YouTube, and you get known that way – you go viral as the Arctic Monkeys did. There's an incredible amount of talent out there.

I So what is your solution to the financial problem?

N Two things. I've contacted the former members of the Burning Pagodas and they've very generously agreed to do a benefit concert in Belmore Park, Sydney – that's near Chinatown – and we hope to raise at least 100,000 dollars.

I And the other thing?

N I'm in touch with the Kuala Lumpur Football Club and I think they'll let us have their stadium for free in July. It holds about 18,000 people, so if we sell tickets at 150 Malaysian Ringgit – that's about 50 dollars – we can gross about 900,000 dollars.

I OK, but you still have overheads.

N Sure, but we can work that out, no problem.

I Last year you had problems with gatecrashers. What do you intend to do about that?

N Well, in a stadium, it's a lot easier to filter people, though they'll probably complain about the queues. We also hope that specialist tour operators will start promoting the festival as well and that'll bring in people from the five continents so the festival will become not just an Asian festival but a truly world festival.

I So what's the line-up this year?

N Top of the bill is Cambodia Dub Foundation. They're a great band and we're bringing back the Java Jive All Stars – they went down very well.

I Who else?

N Well, not entirely sure – it's early days yet – but I've got plenty of contacts.

I OK, Nick, thanks for your time!

N You're welcome.

Unit 8

8.1

1 My name is Ernesto Guerrero. When I left college, there weren't many jobs available and my friends said I should go to temporary employment agencies but I didn't because I wanted a full-time job. I was also reluctant to spend hours on the internet searching online recruitment sites as it's very time-consuming. So I decided to target a number of companies I knew I would want to work for. I sent them my CV and a covering letter but most of them never replied and the ones that did just sent me letters of rejection. Anyway, three months later I contacted one particular company and said why I really wanted to work with them and offered to do a three-month internship without pay. So I think they were impressed by this strategy and they gave me the opportunity to prove myself. And at the end of the three months they took me on.

2 My name is Sofia Baldi and I'm a human resources assistant. I did a first degree in Travel and Tourism and at the same time I joined the Institute for Personnel and Development, which is a professional association for human resources management. They recommended I go to a careers expo and I talked to a few people but it wasn't specifically targeted towards tourism and there wasn't anything specific to personnel management. So, then I took out a subscription to *People Management* magazine. You get a code number and can search their online jobs database and make very specific search requests. That's where I saw my job advertised. I emailed my application and got offered an interview.

3 Hi, I'm Jennifer Willis. I work for a hotel chain as a sales and marketing manager. I graduated from a business school and I thought the best way to find a job would be using professional networking websites like LinkedIn, Plaxo and Ecademy. So I posted my CV on LinkedIn and announced that I was looking for work in the travel industry. I even included a video of myself. But nothing happened. And then a friend who works in IT told me that it is a waste of time sending information about yourself into the black hole of cyberspace if you don't narrow your focus and target specific companies or individual recruiters. He also said that 80 percent of people get their job through recommendation. So, then I started researching hotel chains and following the Twitter feeds of their executives and, sure enough, one of them contacted me, said he liked my profile and offered me a job.

4 My name is Anthony Chan and I first studied Hospitality Management and spent some time working overseas for tour operators, learning how the overseas part of a tour operator's programme works. Then I returned to the UK to be back with my family and I looked after my children while my wife went out to work. When she was made redundant, I started thinking about another position in the hospitality industry. But it was difficult because I had no contacts. I bought a quality newspaper every day but the jobs advertised weren't specific enough. But I was very lucky because one day and quite by chance my wife's uncle, who is based in Hong Kong, got in touch with me and offered me my present post as British representative for a Chinese tour operator.

8.2

1 I'm a human resources manager, so I get to read a large number of CVs and many of them get rejected. Very often, the CV is too long – one A4 page is usually enough – and sometimes it's not printed on good quality paper. It's a very competitive market, so you want to read a CV that stands out from the crowd. So if, under the *Leisure interests* section, a candidate says they like socializing with friends or reading novels, then I'm not really very impressed. It's not a good idea to mention passive, solitary interests like watching TV or playing chess. Hobbies tell the reader something about your personality. For example, if you enjoy mountaineering or whitewater rafting, it shows you have stamina and can stretch yourself to the limit, and that you can depend on your own resources in demanding situations.

2 As a careers advisor, many people ask what my attitude is towards including a photo. Personally, I don't object to seeing a photo but I also see little point in attaching one. In fact, in some countries like the USA it's actively discouraged because it can lead to discrimination. Much more important for me is a description of education and qualifications that I can understand. People often write foreign acronyms or abbreviations like *ESO* or *BTS* that the recruiter can't understand. It's much better to write things like *I did a course in ...*, *I have a degree* – or master's or diploma – *in ...* and then the subject studied. Or *I graduated from the University of wherever in whatever year it was*. But the main thing to remember is that each CV should be tailored to the kind of job you're applying for and contain a *Personal profile* section because I obviously want to match the profile of the person I'm recruiting with the job requirements. It's no good just sending off the same one each time because there's little likelihood of you getting a job if you don't adapt it to the job profile.

3 When I was a student, I did a course at university in writing CVs. The teacher said we should learn expressions to describe our skills and work experience, like *I am good at working under pressure*, *I have a good eye for detail*, *I was responsible for ...*, *I was in charge of ...*, *I specialized in ...* and so on. I also learnt action verbs like *handled*, *designed*, *supervised*, *coordinated*, *monitored* and so on. The first CVs I wrote were very repetitive and had long sentences. I wasn't aware of the need to be concise and use bullet points to list my key accomplishments. I also didn't do any proofreading, so there were spelling and grammatical mistakes I hadn't noticed. I used to think that using colours and different fonts would make my CV stand out but now I know that it doesn't create a good impression – in fact, the opposite – and it's best if it's simple and consistent.

8.3
S = Stephen Lang, I = Interviewer

S What people often don't realize is what they should do before they come for an interview. Obviously, they should anticipate the questions and think about possible answers but there are other things they should do as well. For example, they should find out as much as possible about the company beforehand – for example, the number of employees, the turnover, the structure of the organization, the rates of pay and so on. They should also find out who is actually going to conduct the interview and, if possible, find out about that person's position in the company. Also get the person's mobile phone number.

I Why is that?

S In case there's a problem getting to the interview on time or finding the right office. It can happen.

I How should people dress for an interview?

S First impressions count. In most cases, it's still important for a man to wear a suit and tie and for a woman to be dressed smartly. She should avoid too much jewellery and wear sensible shoes. For both, a trip to the hairdresser a few days before is a good idea. The golden rule is to dress appropriately, neither too casual nor overdressed.

I What's the best way to respond to the interviewer's questions?

S The best way is to show the interviewer what you know by giving specific examples. When you respond with actual on-the-job experiences and situations you've previously had to deal with, you show the interviewer in practical terms what you know and what you can do. Also, you should highlight the skills you've mentioned on your CV and, again, give concrete examples of when and how you used them.

I OK. What about after the interview?

S Well, there's nothing wrong in phoning a few days later to ask whether a decision has been made. It shows you're motivated. But if you don't get the job, you should ask the interviewer why.

I Isn't that kind of impertinent or arrogant?

S Not at all. You need to know so you can make any adjustments next time. You may be able to highlight any weaknesses or maybe there was nothing wrong with you but you just didn't have the right profile.

8.4
S = Stephen Lang, C1 = Candidate 1, C2 = Candidate 2

1

S OK, well, first of all, could you briefly run through your previous experience?

C1 Yes, of course. As you can see from my CV, I did a degree in Travel and Tourism and specialized in events management. I did an internship with a major football club after I graduated and then I got a job on a cruise ship. My duties there were presenting and coordinating activities on board and presenting the on-shore excursion to the passengers at the ports they would visit.

S And what do you think you learnt from that job?

C1 Well, it was very challenging to give talks to hundreds of people, so I had to be really self-confident and well-prepared. So, I think I learnt how important it is to be well-organized; and I needed good communication skills when there were problems with the passengers.

S OK. Can you give me an example of a problem and how you handled it?

C1 Yes, there was once a problem on board ship – there was a hurricane and we couldn't sail into port, so I had to cancel some events and organize different replacement activities for the passengers at short notice. Some of the passengers were unhappy about this, so I had to explain why it was necessary and try to get

them interested in the new activities on offer.

S Could you tell me something about yourself? How would a friend or colleague describe you?

C1 Um ... I guess hard-working and reliable but I'm also creative, good at coming up with ideas and problem-solving.

S Why did you leave your last job?

C1 I didn't leave the job. The job left me.

S You mean you were fired?

C1 No, no, not at all. The cruise line got into financial difficulties and the company had to downsize, so I was made redundant.

2

S Perhaps you could start by telling us something about yourself?

C2 Um ... well ... um ... I like people and I think other people like me. I like working in a team where everybody can contribute and help each other get things done. I'm not afraid of hard work and I think I'm pretty efficient.

S OK. And can you tell us what you find attractive in this particular job?

C2 Well, as you can see from my CV, I've had a number of previous jobs, so I've got quite a lot of experience. Um ... I've never done this kind of job before but, as far as I can tell from the job description, it seems to be one where I can kind of use my skills. And it would also be a good move for me because it would give me better promotion prospects than I had before. Also, I've just got married and we've now bought a flat, so I really need a job to help with the repayments.

S I see that you worked as a telesales representative two years ago. What did you learn from your previous job?

C2 Well, it wasn't easy – the work was very repetitive, which actually is not a bad thing if you're tired, because if you're tired that day, the repetition can kind of help you handle it. Um ... what did I learn? Sometimes the callers are abusive, so you have to have customer service skills, remain calm, you know, be patient and polite. So, yes, I learnt good customer service skills.

S Right. And what would you say is your greatest strength?

C2 Well ... er ... sometimes I've been told that I pay too much attention to detail but I think that's a good thing. As I said, I'm very efficient, so I always make sure that all the paperwork is in order and things get done on time. I think that's important.

S OK. One last question. Can you tell us why we should hire you for this particular job rather than anyone else?

C2 Well, I suppose there are lots of other candidates who could fill this position but I think I'm well-suited to the job description, I'm like ... er ... committed – I know I can do the job well. I'm an efficient kind of person who gets things done.

8.5
S = Stephen Lang, C = Candidate

S Are there any questions you'd like to ask us or any aspects of the job that need clarifying?

C Yes, I've prepared a list of things I'd like to know a bit more about. Um ... first of all, could you tell me something more about what the job involves?

S Yes, you would be working with a team of five other people and your main responsibility would be contacting firms and organizations that would be ready to use our facilities.

C Who would I be reporting to?

S You would be under the day-to-day supervision of your line manager and, ultimately, to the head of department. His name is Herr Grüber and he'll be present at the second interview.

C Uh huh. Um… what kind of training do you offer?

S We have our own Internal Training Department and we regularly organize sessions so that employees can learn any skills they think they lack and go forward to increase their chances of promotion.

C How will my performance be reviewed and who does that?

S There's a first appraisal after three months to discuss how the job is going and then once a year after that. Mr Ross would do that but there's nothing to stop you asking Mrs Wilkins for advice on how well you're doing and any improvements.

8.6

A OK, this post of assistant manager, what's the profile of the person we're looking for?

B Well, I think we need someone with fairly substantial experience, say seven or eight years.

C Not sure about that. This is not a senior position, is it? I'd go for less – three to four.

A OK, so we need a job specification.

C Yeah. So, basically, we're looking for someone who will manage the day-to-day running of the spa. And with responsibility for recruiting a team of beauticians and specialists in wellness treatments.

A Would the person appointed know anything about the spa programme, beauty treatments, thalassotherapy, aromatic plant oils, that sort of thing?

B Well, it would help and I think he or she should provide some assistance in the design and marketing of what the spa offers. But it's not indispensible as we can employ an external consultant to do that.

C Sure – it would be cheaper in-house.

A What about the ideal candidate's previous experience? I guess we're looking for someone with a college or university degree.

B Or higher. And they must be fluent in Spanish. And the ability to use English is strongly recommended.

C I think it's important at this level to have someone who has a good track record in financial management and can make the spa a real going concern. So, the candidate should be good at keeping accurate accounts, providing a good level of customer service and supervising staff. So, excellent people management and communication skills.

A OK, we'll upload the ad this afternoon.

B Just one more thing. We want to grow this business, so it's important for the candidate to really know the spa business. Whoever we appoint should be able to monitor trends in the spa market.

Unit 9

9.1

I = Interviewer, J = Jean-Pierre

I So, Jean-Pierre, what about number 1? Where did the slow food movement originate?

J Ah, I know the answer to this one! The answer's 'Italy'. It was started in 1986 by a man called Carlo Petrini, as a protest against fast food and the opening of a McDonald's near the Spanish steps in Rome. It's now an international movement and aims to preserve traditional and regional cuisine and promote healthy eating habits.

I OK, good start! So how about number 2?

J Well, this is a bit of a trick question. *Fusion* means 'joining two or more things together' but fusion cuisine's not about sauces. The answer is 'd', combinations of cuisines from different regions. A good example would be Tex-Mex.

I So far so good. And number 3?

J Well, as a Frenchman, I'd like the answer to be 'Bordeaux' but, in fact, I know that the answer is 'California'. The San Bernabe vineyard is the biggest grape-growing property in the world, over 3,250 hectares.

I Excellent! I can't imagine you don't know the answer to the next one.

J Well, Dorling Kindersley, Baedeker and Lonely Planet are all guidebooks but only Michelin gives stars to restaurants on the basis of anonymous inspections.

I And number 5?

J *Eggplant* is the word used in the United States, Canada, Australia and New Zealand for *aubergine*. *Zucchini* is the American English word for *courgette*.

I What about tomatoes? Do you know where they originated?

J Yes, they were first grown in South America and brought to Europe by the Spanish. They were originally called 'xitomatl', which, apparently, meant 'the swelling fruit'.

I OK, the next four questions are all about the names of internationally famous dishes. Which of them do you know?

J Bouillabaisse is easy. It's a delicious fish stew from Marseille in southeast France. For number 8, all these dishes are made from cheese – a croque monsieur, for example, is basically a toasted cheese sandwich – but the only one from Switzerland is the fondue, which is a dish of melted cheese served in a big pot and eaten by dipping bread into it on the end of a long fork.

I Right. And number 9?

J I'm not sure. I hesitate between Mexico and Brazil for the guacamole. I'll go for Brazil.

I Oh, sorry! Guacamole originated with the Aztecs in Mexico. So you got one wrong there!

J Oh dear, not good for my reputation! But I do recognize these dishes. We've got sushi from Japan and moules frites, that is mussels and French fries, from Belgium. It's interesting that French fries probably aren't French at all – the word *frenching* refers to the technique of cutting something into long strips. And, of course, in Britain

they're actually called chips, not fries.

I And the last photo?

J Um … that looks like a borscht, which is a beetroot soup and very popular in Russia and across eastern Europe.

I Excellent! So, almost full marks for the quiz! Well, now I'd like us to talk a little bit about …

9.2

W = Waiter, D1 = Diner 1, D2 = Diner 2

W Are you ready to order?

D1 Hi, could you just tell us what these dishes are? For example, what's the kuzu pirzola?

W OK, these are tender lamb cutlets which are marinated in red pepper, then grilled over charcoal and served with rice.

D1 Sounds good. And what about lahmacun?

W That's a kind of Turkish pizza. There's a round bread base that's baked in a brick oven and topped with minced meat, tomatoes and herbs.

D1 That sounds delicious. I'll have that.

W And Madam?

D2 What's the levrek pilaki?

W It's a tasty stew made by simmering fish with carrots and tomatoes, and flavoured with onions and garlic.

D2 And what's it served with?

W Potatoes.

D2 OK. And this one? Midye dolmasi?

W That's a delicious dish of fresh mussels, which are stuffed with a spicy rice mixture, steamed over a low fire and accompanied by chopped shallots.

9.3

1 The way we were treated was absolutely awful! The waiters were in an extremely bad mood, shouting at each other and generally annoying us. And when we tried to catch their eye to ask for something, they totally ignored us!

2 I don't often go to an Indian restaurant but when I do, I expect to hear sitars or maybe there's a video of some Bollywood movie but the last one I went to was playing Chopin!

3 When you go to an Italian restaurant, you expect to see something that reminds you of Italy – an Italian flag, pictures of Florence and Rome, red and white chequered tablecloths with matching napkins and green napkin rings … This one just had a huge picture of Bob Marley on the wall! I like reggae very much but what's this got to do with Italy?

4 This restaurant is so popular but, in fact, I would never go there because unless you get there first thing in the evening, you'll probably have to stand in a long queue on the pavement until someone decides to leave. I don't understand why they don't take reservations.

5 There was no dish of the day or house speciality – just four kinds of salad that looked and tasted identical and the kind of courses you'd expect in any Greek taverna.

6 The perfect place for a romantic dinner by candlelight, with waiters dressed in traditional black and white to capture the ambience of 19th-century Paris.

7 I nearly had a heart attack when the waiter, who had a big smile on his face, ive me the bill! I'd recommend this restaurant on condition that you take out a bank loan beforehand!

9.4

M = Manager, W1 = Waiter 1,
W2 = Waiter 2, W3 = Waiter 3

M Can everyone come here, please? I've just been reading the customer reviews we've had over the last few days and, first of all, I'm pleased to say that most customers think the quality of food here is really good, so congratulations to the chef. On the other hand, it seems the quality of service sometimes leaves a lot to be desired. Apparently, one of you, I won't mention names, has been getting the orders wrong. So could you please make sure that you double-check what the customer has ordered and preferably write it down?

W1 But we've run out of note pads!

M Well, OK, if that's the case, I'll order some more. But just make sure you get the order right. We had a customer who ordered a drink with lemon and there was no lemon. Honestly, it's not complicated!

W2 But we don't have any lemons. They weren't in the last delivery.

M Why are we always running out of things? Another customer complained that there was no guacamole. Mercedes, you're in charge of inventory. Please make sure that we keep enough of everything in stock so it won't happen again.

W2 OK.

M Another thing: can you tell me, why are customers having to wait so long to get served?

W3 We don't have enough people. There are lots of customers, two of the kitchen staff are off sick – it's difficult. Alamar didn't come on Monday.

M But why not?

W3 I don't know.

M Well, I need to know these things! I wasn't here last week. If there's a problem, get in touch with me ASAP. You all have my mobile number, don't you?

ALL No.

M What? OK, I'll write it down and give it to you again. Well, finally, on a more positive note, I see from the reviews that you've been attentive to the customers and asking them if they're satisfied. That's really good and that's what we said in the last feedback session. But be careful: don't give them the impression that you're harassing them. Just ask them first if they're satisfied with their meal and then try and judge when exactly your service is needed. OK, everybody, that's all for now. Keep up the good work and enjoy the rest of the day!

9.5

I = Interviewer, R = Rosa

I So, Rosa, how was it that you first got interested in creating a gastronomic tour in Peru?

R Well, two years ago I visited the Mistura food festival in Lima and I came away very excited. It's the largest food fair in Latin America, with more than 650,000 visitors. And as regards regional cuisine, Peru has the same status as France does in Europe.

My husband and I had just sold our last travel business and we had some money to invest. We thought the next big thing would be culinary tours and Peruvian cuisine, so we set out to find out more.

I And what did you discover?

R Well, the great thing about Peruvian cuisine is its ability to incorporate gastronomic influences from so many different cultures. I mean, the Incas gave us the potato but also cereals like quinoa and meat like the alpaca. And then the Spanish introduced olives, grapes, dairy products and rice and the two cuisines began to fuse, so there are dishes that combine the best of both worlds, like papa a la huancaína, which is basically boiled potatoes in a spicy, creamy sauce.

I OK, but I've heard that the real gastronomic revolution arrived from the Far East.

R That's right. Both the Chinese and the Japanese were employed as cheap labour in the cotton and sugar plantations. At the beginning of the 19th century, 100,000 Chinese immigrants arrived in Peru and their influence is felt in the number of Chinese restaurants, called 'chifas'. There are over 2,000 of them.

I And the Japanese?

R They came to Peru for the same reason and brought with them a taste for seafood which the Peruvians didn't have. Our national dishes of tiradito and ceviche are based on raw fish and owe a lot to the Japanese culinary tradition.

9.6

R = Rosa, L = Luis

R OK, Luis, you've read the comments and we've talked a bit about reworking the itinerary. What are your conclusions?

L Well, I think we should focus more on the culinary experience. We should do more visits to restaurants and tastings with local chefs. For example, we should offer a Peruvian fusion experience at the Astrid y Gaston. I know the chef there and he will do tastings. And we must teach them to cook an Inca Pachamanca on hot stones.

R Yeah, that's a good idea. And I can get in touch with the chef at A Puerto Cerrada and do a tasting of creole cuisine. He does a really good buffet lunch, which everyone would enjoy. And there's also the Japanese fusion place, Toshiro's – that's well worth a visit.

L Maybe more visits to local farmers' markets to sample local produce. We could hire an interpreter and talk to some of the local farmers and growers.

R What about the Mistura? It seems people want to stay longer.

L Yes, but I'm not sure people would want to go to too many seminars or conferences. The main thing is to let them spend enough time to sample everything. I guess real foodies can only do the event justice by buying a multi-day ticket and coming every day for breakfast, lunch and dinner.

R What about the other non-food activities?

L There's so much to do. For example, the

Pachacamac Sun Temple is only half an hour away and we could do a tour of Lima by night. And if people want to go further afield to Machu Picchu or Chiclayo, we can put those on as optional extras.

Unit 10

10.1

I = Interviewer, L = Lisa

I First of all, can you tell us about the best practices you've put in place to anticipate the risks that may occur in any of your destinations?

L Well, yes, we have a risk management strategy that we use to identify and hopefully prevent the likelihood of any disaster in a particular context, although, of course, some natural disasters can't be foreseen. The first stage is to identify the source of risk, and the nature and scope of issues that we need to address in order to ensure the safety of the destination.

I Can you give us some examples?

L Well, in some countries there is the possibility of an earthquake, some countries have a particularly high crime rate, some countries are prone to civil unrest, strikes or rioting. So, we develop risk statements such as *There is a risk that flooding within the town of X will inundate Hotel Y. Or There is a high risk of personal injury associated with this or that adventure sport.* Then we analyze the risks in the destination and evaluate them in terms of their impact: severe, high, moderate or low – their frequency, their likely duration and their scope. Will a disaster be of limited duration, like an explosion, or last a significant length of time, like an epidemic or a flood? And, from a tourism perspective, will the risk affect just one operator or a whole destination? So, we have to be proactive, brainstorm all the risks that we can possibly think of and prioritize them in order of importance.

I So, 'identify', 'analyze', 'evaluate'. What about 'treat'?

L Well, as I said before, you can't prevent all risks but there are a number of options. You can avoid the risk by, for example, not using a hotel situated on a flood plain or not offering a particularly dangerous adventure activity. You can lessen the likelihood of a threat by putting in place adequate systems both for the traditional hazards, such as a fire or a cyclone, for example, and also new threats, such as information security: organized crime networks will inevitably try to get access to the information we hold about our clients, the credit card information and so on, so we have to make sure that all that information is fully secure.

I How many people should be involved in this process?

L Risk management is a team effort; it's not just one particular person's job, so we set up a crisis planning committee with representatives of every department. We also consult representatives from all the key stakeholders in the local community as each of them will have a different perspective, and unique skills and knowledge to contribute. And given that risks are rarely static, it is important to monitor and review the risk management plan on a regular basis, ideally, every three months, so that everybody knows what to do and when.

10.2

... and news is coming in of an accident at the ski resort at Beaver Ridge, Colorado. Apparently, some time after seven o'clock, when the resort had closed for the day, a 12-year-old girl was severely injured after her sled hit a snow groomer at the bottom of the beginner slope. Her nine-year-old brother was also riding on the sled but managed to throw himself clear before the sled hit the machine.

The circumstances of the accident are unclear but, apparently, the snow groomer was travelling at 19 kilometres an hour and heading towards the snow bridge when the girl emerged from behind the ski lift and lost control of her wooden sled.

The driver of the snow groomer, a recently-recruited man aged 44, was being questioned by police to clarify the circumstances of the accident. According to our information, he has a heart condition and may have been taken ill after failing to take his medication. Keep tuned for an update. This is Caroline Johnson at WCTB, for news on the hour, every hour.

10.3

A Would you say that most travel companies are sufficiently prepared to cope with an emergency?

B No, not really. There's a lot of talk in the adventure travel business about risk evaluation but, in fact, many companies just don't see it as a priority. And that's wrong because your customer could be on a villa holiday in Italy or Turkey and there's an earthquake – the risks are the same.

C Yeah, and in an emergency it's your company's reputation on the line. If you want to be doing business next month, you need a crisis response.

D I think the most important thing is briefing your staff and running a simulation. A lot of it comes down to practical issues like who is going to take charge and who is going to man the phones.

B Yeah, you need to train staff on how to deal with anxious families and friends, the media and clients on the ground.

D The first hour is the most important; we call it the golden hour. It's the most critical because you have to evaluate how serious the situation is and take all the measures that you've already put in place. And it's always better to be safe than sorry.

B We have yellow, orange and red levels of crisis. We decide which level it is and then carry out an action plan depending on the nature of the crisis.

C And you need all that contact information for next of kin as news travels fast and we prefer to get in touch with relatives before they get in touch with us. But how many companies actually have that next of kin information at their fingertips?

D Right. And technology has made this first hour even more crucial, as people on holiday will often make phone calls or film videos at the scene and upload them onto the internet before the operator is even aware of the crisis.

C I remember when there was a bus crash in South Africa in 2010, just two days before the World Cup. The company asked a social networking site to take down pictures and comments because they were distressing relatives.

B That's true. But regular updates on your own website or text messages are a very important way of getting information to clients and their families very quickly.

C Communication is the key and if you get it right, a well-handled emergency could actually help you to generate more business.

10.4

A Well, everybody is congratulating you on having been chosen for the next Olympic Games. But what do you see as the real benefits of having been selected?

B Yes, we're all very excited but it's going to be a lot of hard work between now and then to make the games truly successful. But there are enormous benefits. First of all, national pride. The games bring people together, they create a real sense of community; people are proud when the whole world is watching their country and there's a great atmosphere. Secondly, there's a huge benefit in creating the facilities for the games: new transport links, new sports stadiums and all the amenities for the athletes themselves.

A Isn't there a risk these will cost a fortune and not be used afterwards, so, eventually, it's the taxpayer who has to foot the bill?

B No, all the facilities will be used by local people and the accommodation for the athletes will be converted into social housing. And there will be a major spin-off in terms of urban regeneration. There will be a lot of work done in run-down areas that need investment and so many of the events will be held in these areas. Of course, that means that a lot of jobs will be created as well.

A OK, and I suppose the revenue from tourism will help meet the costs.

B Sure. Thousands of extra visitors are bound to help the tourism sector – both in the short and long term – in raising the profile of the country.

A Great! Well, we're all looking forward to the opening ceremony!